D0184337

Horse Driving Trials

Horse Driving Trials

The Sport of Competitive Coachmanship

Tom Coombs

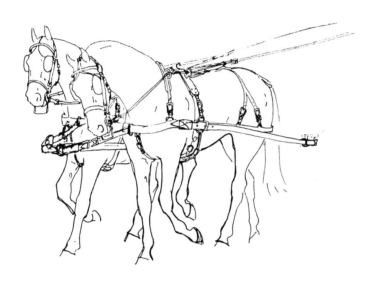

DAVID & CHARLES
Newton Abbot   London   North Pomfret (Vt)

The author would like to thank all those who have
supplied photographs for this book

Line illustrations by Joy Claxton
Cartoons by John Tickner

British Library Cataloguing in Publication Data

Coombs, Tom
 Horse driving trials
 1. Driving of horse-drawn vehicles
 I. Title
 798'.6   SF305

 ISBN 0-7153-8732-4

Typeset by ABM Typographics Limited, Hull
and printed in Great Britain
by Redwood Burn Limited, Trowbridge, Wilts
for David & Charles (Publishers) Limited
Brunel House   Newton Abbot   Devon

Published in the United States of America
by David & Charles Inc
North Pomfret   Vermont 05053   USA

Dedication

This book is dedicated with affectionate respect to Mr Bernard Mills, who almost bridges the gap in time between horse transport and horse driving trials. As chairman of the first British Driving Trials Committee, he guided our faltering footsteps into competition driving with the same elegant and efficient assurance that he always displayed on the box seat of his own coach. His innate courtesy and good humour have endeared him to all driving enthusiasts in Britain and the many representatives of other nations with whom he worked so tirelessly and successfully to establish driving trials as a major international horse sport.

Preface

Two enterprising girls who worked for the publishers inspired this book and encouraged me to write it. I tackled the task in the knowledge that two very good books had already been published about competition driving: one in England by the Duke of Edinburgh and the other in America by Mr Emil Bernard Jung. These are written by top-class competitors for competitors and, although Prince Philip's sportingly light-hearted account of his own progress to the top of the international driving tree is great fun for anyone to read, they can both rightly be regarded as textbooks which should be studied by all trials drivers who aspire to excel at the sport. This offering is not a textbook but rather an appreciation of all that is involved in driving trials.

Competitors will find here advice about the solving of some of the many problems which confront them when they contemplate taking up the sport and want to do well at it, but I have also sought to outline the duties and responsibilities of the many other people whose less prominent participation is essential to the successful conduct of a driving event. Spectators of driving trials seem quickly to become active supporters and they may find in this book some of the answers to some of the questions which they want to ask about becoming more closely and actively involved.

I have been given much food for thought by the many enthusiasts who have asked questions of me and expressed their opinions; some of the latter though being controversial and even contentious have been none the less interesting and sometimes valuable as pointers to desirable reforms. I am most grateful to the editors of *Horse and Hound, Horse & Driving* and *In Memoriam Achenbach* who have always provided me with a forum from which I have been able to give replies to questions and recommendations on a much wider basis than would ever have been possible in conversation or private correspondence, and this book is another one.

I stopped driving a four-in-hand just before driving trials in their present form started and, being plunged immediately and most enjoyably into the judging and administration of them, have never been seriously tempted to risk my neck or my purse as a competitor. I reckon that I have had about half as much fun as a competitor has, but about three times as often and at far less expense. I am eternally grateful to all the competitors who have so generously allowed me to maintain the conceit that I could have matched any of their skills if I had got round to having a go myself.

Contents

1
Origins and Outline

'She must have heard you call her Boadicea the first time round.'

People have been travelling in carts pulled by horses for about five thousand years, although in some early civilisations, such as the Sumerian kingdom of 3000BC, the carts were more often pulled by large asses called onagers because these were stronger and faster than the small ponies available at the time. By contrast, people started making journeys on horseback only about 1,500 years ago because before then the horses were not really big enough and stirrups had not been invented. Attila the Hun is credited with having introduced stirrups in about AD450 and although it may have been almost his only beneficence to mankind it was undoubtedly a significant one. Anyone who doubts this should try riding an Exmoor pony for twenty miles or so with just a blanket strapped to its back to get an idea of what riding was like 1,500 years ago.

Driving, however, was a faster and more efficient form of travel in the distant past, and history relates that envoys and couriers travelled regularly between London and Rome in the days of the Roman Empire, taking an average of only thirteen days to make the journey. They did this in relays of chariots pulled by two or four ponies with skilled professional drivers in stages of between eight and fifteen miles over the good Roman roads and, since the distance is about 1,300 miles, they averaged about a hundred miles a day.

A more recent historical record from the nineteenth century reveals that when Sir Robert Peel was sent for by Queen Victoria to return from Rome to London the journey took him rather longer than thirteen days, despite the fact that a summons from the Queen brooked no delay and every possible effort was made to speed his progress. The Roman record for regular long distance overland travel thus probably stood until it was challenged by the English mail coaches in the nineteenth century. They averaged 9–10mph during the short-lived 'golden age of coaching', but were almost immediately superseded by the railways.

When the Roman roads fell into disuse, in about AD500, wheeled transport became largely impractical throughout most of Western Europe and everyone walked or rode; the infirm were carried in litters slung between two led horses, if they could afford it. Further east, where steppes and plains predominated over forests and marshes, people could still drive, quite fast in two-wheeled chariots or sleighs over the snow or slowly in four-wheeled waggons which could not turn corners because they lacked the forecarriage or 'fifth wheel' which had not yet been invented.

The coach as such originated in the fifteenth century in the town of Kocs in Hungary from which it took its name. As a four-wheeled vehicle, it was distinguished from the slow, clumsy waggons which preceded it by having a forecarriage on which the front wheels and their axle could be turned horizontally for steering, and rudimentary springing for the comfort of passengers and to prevent it shaking to pieces at fast paces over rough ground. Coaches, lighter four-wheeled carriages, and two-wheeled carts with springs made their appearance in England by the beginning of the seventeenth century but were not able to travel over the whole country until the end of the eighteenth century when the good roads made by Metcalfe, Telford and Macadam made this possible. These vehicles reigned supreme in providing all public and most private transport throughout Western Europe until the railways took over the long journeys between major cities by the middle of the nineteenth century, and were still essential for getting to the station until motor transport became available at the beginning of the twentieth century.

The Great War of 1914–18 effectively put an end to carriage driving in Western Europe; most of the horses and their coachmen went to the front and those of the latter who returned became chauffeurs. Carriage driving became virtually obsolete for over thirty years until the coronation of Queen Elizabeth II in 1952. For this Colonel Arthur Main, Captain Frank Gilbey, Mr Sanders Watney and Mr Reg Brown, all now sadly deceased, produced a magnificent procession of carriages, all horsed and driven by amateurs. They used this initiative to found the British Driving Society, whose membership has now grown to over four thousand; and there must now be some five thousand horse-drawn vehicles in use in Britain, including about twenty four-horse coaches, which have assembled for meets of the Coaching Club on several occasions during this decade.

Horse-drawn transport lasted longer in Eastern Europe, where petrol and mechanical technology were in shorter supply, and has always survived in the rural areas of the American continent, in some cases for religious reasons as with the Amish people in Pennsylvania.

Howlett and Achenbach

The state studs of Hungary, Poland, Czechoslovakia and Germany have always maintained the skill of driving four-horse teams as part of their training routines; and in Germany and Switzerland this has been perpetuated as an art and a competitive endeavour largely because of the influence of Benno von Achenbach (1861–1936) and his disciple Max Pape, who died in 1977. Benno von Achenbach owed much of his inspiration and early training to Edwin Howlett, an English coachman who taught the art of four-horse driving to many distinguished pupils, including the American Fairman Rogers, in Paris at the turn of the last century. Howlett was the first person to teach four-in-hand driving as an artistic skill rather than just a manual trade, and Achenbach and Pape, being confirmed anglophiles, always generously conceded his influence on their achievements. Thus has developed the Achenbach or English style of driving with its links back to the Prince Regent, 'the first gentleman of Europe', who first adopted and promoted such driving as a Corinthian pursuit. The final link, more direct if perhaps fortuitous, is forward to the Duke of Edinburgh who, as today's 'first gentleman of

13

Europe', at least in equestrian circles, has taken on the reins from his royal predecessor and handles them much more skilfully.

The Start of International Driving Trials

The Duke of Edinburgh, as president of the International Equestrian Federation (FEI), visited the great International Horse Show at Aachen in 1968 and was impressed by the twenty or so four-in-hands which he saw there competing against one another in performance trials through obstacles. He responded with enthusiasm to the suggestion of Mr Eric Brabec, secretary-general of the Polish Equestrian Federation, that this sport should be organised internationally, and made immediate arrangements to this effect, determining at the same time to take it up himself as an eventual replacement for polo.

Prince Philip's initiative bore instant fruit and international rules for driving trials were published within a year, enabling the first international event to take place in Switzerland in 1970. This was followed by European Championships in Hungary in 1971 and World Championships in Germany in 1972, and since then World Championships have taken place in each year of even date, alternating with European Championships in the intervening years until 1983 when championships for pairs were substituted for the European four-horse championships.

To date (spring 1985), World Championships have taken place in Germany (1972), Switzerland (1974), Holland (1976), Hungary (1978), England (1980), Holland (1982), and Hungary (1984). European Championships have taken place in Hungary (1971), England (1973), Poland (1975), Germany (1977), France (1979), and Switzerland (1981).

The first European Championships for pairs were held in Italy in 1983 and the first World Pairs Championships will be in England in 1985. The 1986 World Championships are also scheduled to be held in England.

Cynthia Hayden driving Mr McDougald's team of Hackneys in the 1974 World Championships in Switzerland *(Findlay Davidson)*

The Events

Today's driving trials follow closely the format of the ridden three-day event with one extra competition added: this is presentation, an assessment of the turnout and general quality of each competitor's ensemble judged at the halt just before the dressage on the first day. Their composition therefore is: Competition AI, presentation, followed on the same day by Competition AII, dressage; Competition B, marathon, comparable to the speed and endurance phase of ridden horse trials; and Competition C, obstacle driving, which replaces the show jumping competition.

The rules allow for any of these competitions to be held separately, but together they form 'a combined driving event', and the order in which they take place may be altered in certain circumstances. Competition B, the marathon, is however always regarded as the most important phase and the system of scoring takes this into account in according it the greatest influence.

Since the general aim is to prove the best all-round combination of horse(s) and driver, trials almost invariably comprise all three competitions, but the full marathon of five sections covering a total distance of 27km may be reduced down to one section to allow an event to be held in two days, or only one.

The Three Competitions

The three competitions, which are described in detail in later chapters, together provide a forum for drivers to demonstrate the full range of their horses' qualities and capabilities and their own skills.

In Competition AI the condition of the whole turnout, including the driver and groom(s), is examined. In Competition AII the driver demonstrates his own skill in precise rein handling and the obedience, good manners and free and regular paces of his horse(s).

Competition B tests the speed, stamina and courageous intelligence of the horses and the skill and judgement of the drivers. Competition C proves that the horses are still willing and agile after their previous day's exertions and requires meticulous accuracy on the part of the drivers.

The Scurry Competition

Competition C, the obstacle competition, can be judged on time in the same way as a speed competition in show jumping. In this form it frequently takes place by itself as a ring attraction at horse shows where it has come to be known as a 'scurry competition'.

Scurry competitions are in effect an offshoot of driving trials and have become popular, particularly in Britain, to fill intervals between show jumping classes. Confined to pairs of ponies, they are easy to stage and exciting to watch, being the modern equivalent of chariot racing. Equestrian purists condemn these competitions as being indecorous and the antithesis of horsemanship but, although the ponies which take part in them quickly become too hot and excitable for anything else, they add an extra entertainment to the horse show scene and help to publicise their parent activity.

The Rules for Pairs, Singles and Ponies

The original rules were drawn up for teams of four horses and to win with one of these must surely be the summit of the ambition of any competitive driver who can afford to keep one. However, international trials for pony teams have taken place in England, Holland and Germany, and we now have World Championships for horse pairs. All national trials in Britain, and most of them in Western Europe, America and Australia, include classes for pairs, tandems and singles as well as four-in-hands, and for ponies as well as horses, but there are not many tandems or horses driven in single harness in Eastern Europe, nor are there many ponies, although these are beginning to make their appearance in Hungary.

The international height limit for ponies is 148cm (14.2hh) so that the range of size for ponies is nearly twice that for horses. This is appreciated, particularly in Britain where many Welsh Mountain ponies and some Shetlands compete regularly, but event organisers are seldom willing to put on special classes for ponies under 12.2hh, or under 12hh, so these have to compete against much bigger animals and, to their credit, quite often beat them. To subdivide the usual four pony classes would create an extra four classes, making twelve in all, and this would either make too many entries in total or not enough in each class.

Ponies seem to be, remarkably, stronger in relation to their height than horses because, whereas pairs of ponies up to 14.2hh are required to pull a carriage weighing at least 225kg (4½ cwt) as compared with 350kg (7cwt) for pairs of horses (200kg (4cwt) and 300kg (6 cwt) respectively under British national rules), pairs of ponies 12.2hh or less get no weight concession for being so much smaller.

17

Colonel Sir John Miller, the Crown Equerry, driving the Queen's grey Olden-burg team in the first International Driving Championships in 1970 *(Findlay Davidson)*

In fact it is difficult to build a four-wheeled carriage, however small, which is strong enough for a marathon and weighs less than 200kg (4cwt), and in the case of two-wheeled carts for single ponies and horses, whose required weights are 90kg (1¾cwt) and 150kg (3cwt) respectively under British national rules, it is impossible to build one which is strong enough and weighs less than 90kg (1¾cwt). Therefore, Shetland ponies, which normally weigh less than their carts and the two people in them, are discouraged from competing in single harness, although they have been successful in pair harness and a tandem of Shetlands has performed very well.

International Events

In the northern hemisphere fifteen European nations and the United States of America currently compete in driving trials. Australia and South Africa run their own trials but cannot compete internationally because of distance and quarantine regulations.

International championships are open to national teams of three entries plus two individual entries, with the host nation permitted to enter a greater number of individuals. The scores of the best two team members in each competition, provided that none is eliminated, decide the team championships, so that a national team may consist of only two entries. The number of individual entries permitted in addition to national teams is variable and depends on the total number of entries, which cannot reasonably exceed fifty so long as the present (1985) rules for these championships are in force. A nation is permitted to make just one individual entry for a World Championship.

Other international trials, not having championship status, are held in most European countries each year and the significant difference is that the host nation is not obliged to pay all the expenses of the foreign competitors while they are in their country. Some of these events, notably those at Aachen and Hamburg in Germany and Deurne in Holland, and the Danube/Alpine trials, are open to specified numbers of competitors from any nation.

At Royal Windsor Show each year in May a driving Grand Prix is held to which some foreign four-horse teams and pairs are invited, and classes for pony teams and pairs are also included to which competitors from overseas are invited.

The bulletin of the International Equestrian Federation listed nineteen international driving events for Europe for 1985, including the World Pairs Championships and the Royal Windsor Driving Grand Prix in England.

Trials in Britain

The British Horse Society listed fifteen official national fixtures for 1985 including the two mentioned above and the two annual events at Scone and Kelso in Scotland. At least forty small events, mostly just one-day ones, are also run in Britain each year by clubs. These clubs have a local or regional membership and in 1985 there were fourteen of them, specialising in driving trials and affiliated to the Driving Trials Group of the British Horse Society, and many more general driving clubs, not necessarily affiliated, running a few competitions based on driving trials' rules.

All these clubs do a good job in giving people the opportunity to have an inexpensive taste of competition driving in a friendly informal atmosphere within easy reach of their own homes. They contrive to run their events at very low cost, covered by their members' subscriptions and modest entry fees, and prize winners are content to receive only rosettes.

As an example, the Midlands Driving Trials Group, with almost two hundred members, runs seven events each summer at different locations throughout the Midlands and East Anglia, with an average of seventy entries at each, and none of them has cost the group more than £200 to put on. The contrast is with a World Championship which must budget to spend at least £75,000.

Spectator Appeal

The appeal of driving trials as a spectator sport is clearly limited, at least in Britain where the abundance of race meetings, horse shows and other competitive horse activities makes audiences sophisticated to the point of being blasé.

Dressage is tediously mystifying for the uninitiated to watch, such excitements as the marathon offers are unpredictable and missed by most of the people who have come to see them, and the obstacle competition in its present form, unless held as a separate scurry competition, is hardly an exciting arena attraction.

Driving events attract supporters rather than spectators: people who prefer to walk about and associate with competitors and their horses rather than to be marshalled into stands and enclosures and watch pre-arranged performances. The number of supporters increases steadily at each event each year and the trials at Lowther, which have been held since 1973 and are now run in conjunction with an impressive country fair, check about twenty thousand people through their gates and are almost uncomfortably crowded.

There is good television to be made at driving trials — and several national programmes have been presented and much appreciated — as well as a wealth of commercial and private video films. Since there is no betting involved and no great anxiety to know immediate results, these appeal to an eventual armchair audience which is incalculable but considerable and certainly growing.

Imre Abonyi, the first Hungarian World Champion, driving his team of Lippizzaner cross Orlov Trotters in the European Championships, Windsor, 1973 *(Findlay Davidson)*

The Cost and the Sponsor

Since nearly all British driving trials are held in large parks and private estates which do not normally cater for large influxes of visitors, the cost of providing temporary public facilities is high. A 'chicken and egg' situation tends to result in that trials organisers seek commercial sponsorship in order to be able to budget for a big impressive event, and sponsors understandably demand expensive arrangements to attract and cater for a big public attendance.

Much of the sponsors' money must be spent on the provision of public facilities and this may seem to have been wasted if the public, who are greatly influenced by the weather, do not come to the event. It is difficult to balance these requirements so long as it is impossible to forecast 'the gate', and all too easy to create the impression that competition driving is an expensive recreation which consists of rich people displaying their extravagances to one another.

21

Flexibility within the Rules

The rules do not encourage cost cutting by organisers or competitors and are not devised to provide entertainment for spectators. However, after a few astonishing misconceptions were sorted out, such as that which equated the process of a carriage being reversed in negotiating a marathon obstacle with a refusal by a horse at a fence, and penalised it accordingly, they now form a reasonable basis for assessing the qualities of harness horses and the skills of their drivers. The preamble and introduction to the international rules concede that they do not cover all eventualities and are not intended to impose rigid standardisation. They recommend that the rules must be strictly enforced so as to be fair for all, but that there is scope within them for organisers to use their initiative to keep competitors happy and spectators amused.

The international rules are amended annually and have been reprinted every four years. The British national rules copy them in all essentials but contain some extra provisions for tandems and single turnouts and to suit arrangements for events which do not last for three days but still cater for fifty or more entries.

The rules of racing have been in existence for well over two hundred years and are still revised and amended annually. It is not surprising that the rules of driving trials need altering just as often and, provided that this is done with due regard for all the effects which alterations will have and not just the immediate ones, and so long as the alterations are correctly translated into all the relevant languages, the sport will grow in probity and efficacy year by year.

George Bowman with his Welsh Cob team in the Windsor Grand Prix. The author is sitting beside him as referee *(Findlay Davidson)*

2
Presentation

'You're not in the car now. There's no need for back-seat driving!'

The object of the presentation, Competition Section AI, is to judge the turnout, cleanliness, condition and general impression of the horses, driver and grooms, harness and vehicle. This sentence, taken straight from the international rules, describes very adequately what the competition consists of and, by implication, why it is included in driving trials, but the justification for presentation is less obvious and has been a matter of perennial controversy.

Being an assessment purely of appearance and judged only at the halt, it is unique as a part of any performance trials and considered by its critics to be out of place in them. Its critics also assert that success in presentation can be bought and requires no skill or effort on the part of a driver or his horses; they maintain that it is liable to be judged unfairly because standards vary widely between different judges and there can be no common criterion by which to evaluate the many different styles of turnout which are presented at international and even national trials. A fair proportion of regular competitors in Britain and all other countries have, however, always supported the concept of presentation. These have by no means been only those who have been able to afford the most expensive carriages, harness, appointments and paid grooms, and the number and proportion of such supporters has grown considerably in recent years, so that presentation is now generally accepted and is clearly a permanent feature of all driving trials. It is amply justified, in the opinion of those who agree with it, on two counts:

1 In the best traditions of all countries, an elegant, well-polished and well-cared-for appearance has always been an intrinsic quality in any horse-drawn carriage, whether state or sporting, and the achievement of this in respect of the whole turnout has always excited rivalry between owners and their coachmen.

2 Demonstrations of driving skill and the ability and state of training of horses do not have much spectator appeal in themselves since they do not amount to absolute tests of speed or agility and do not create the excitement engendered by close-fought rivalry as in races. The sparkle and glamour with which competitors have invested the first and last days of modern driving trials have been largely induced by their competitive efforts in presentation, and have created carnival atmospheres which have attracted spectators and brought to these events the public recognition on which they depend for their financial support. It is significant that the excellently devised driving tests which have been held in Germany for the past sixty years, and which could be seen at horse shows there before the advent of driving trials, are virtually unknown except to their own exponents and devotees. These, though judged against a standard for the award of gold, silver and bronze medals rather than competitively, are critical tests of coachmanship but, since turnout plays no part in them and is only utilitarian, very few people want to watch them and will not pay to do so. By the same token, the British Driving Society holds proficiency tests almost every week but does not expect spectators to attend them.

Competition A — Section I
PRESENTATION

COMPETITOR NO	TO BE JUDGED	MARKS 1 — 10	REMARKS
1. Driver, Groom and Passengers	Position, dress, hat, gloves, holding whip, handling of horses.		
2. Horses	Condition, turn out, cleanliness, matching, condition of shoeing.		
3. Harness	Condition, proper fit, cleanliness.		
4. Vehicle	Condition, cleanliness, height of pole and spare equipment.		
5. General Impression	Whole turnout.		
	TOTAL PRESENTATION		

SIGNATURE OF JUDGE ....

Judging sheet for Competition A – Section 1 – Presentation

Judging and Scoring

The requirements for presentation are set out in the facsimile of the judging sheet shown above. The scale of marks is the same as that for judging dressage, with each mark denoting an opinion of the judge who gives it. Judging is against a standard and not comparative between competitors, and judges must be careful to maintain their standards throughout a competition, or at least a class. They must not yield to the temptation of judging arithmetically by forgetting what the marks actually mean and thinking to give 'one more or one less mark' according to faults found or whether the competitor they are currently judging seems slightly better or slightly worse than the one before. For the same reason, fractions of marks may not be given.

A slight variation of standards between different judges is unavoidable and quite permissible, but three judges should be employed as often as possible, and always at important events, so that one whose standards are significantly out of line may be more easily revealed. 'Excellent', for 10 marks, may properly be regarded as denoting hypothetical perfection which is seldom if ever encountered in any of the requirements for presentation, but the general standard, at least in

Britain, is now so high that most competitors merit a rating of 'good' or 'very good' under all the five headings. A rating of only 'fairly good', for 7 marks, is unusual, only 'satisfactory', for 6, is rare and less than this is now almost unheard of.

Judges are expected to write on their sheets any comments about faults or shortcomings which have influenced their ratings and must do this to support any rating of 'less than satisfactory'. However, they can hardly be expected to state in writing why any aspect of a turnout seems to them to be only fairly good or good rather than very good and it is quite in order for them to make verbal recommendations to competitors about minor improvements which would please them, but not really alter the gradings which they give.

To arrive at a score expressed in penalty points, the total bonus marks from each judge are divided by the number of judges, which is never more than three, and subtracted from the 'possible' of 50 for each competitor. They should be recorded to the first decimal point and at national trials in Britain are further reduced so as to lessen the influence of presentation on the final results of an event. Prior to 1985 they were halved to achieve this, but from 1985 onwards it is likely that the total bonus marks of the three judges and the total possible marks they can give will be divided by 5 to achieve a similar, but normally greater, reduction after the subtraction is made. Thus, if a competitor is given 42, 38 and 45 marks respectively by each of the three judges, his final penalty mark will be 9 out of 10, which is 1 penalty.

Before writing about the detailed requirements of this competition I should like to introduce a personal note. As a judge, my own yardstick for assessing whether a turnout is correct and suitable or not is that the whole turnout must impress me as displaying traditional and functional elegance and every separate component of it must seem to display two of these qualities but not necessarily, or usually, all three of them. For instance: carriage lamps are traditional and elegant but by no means functional nowadays in comparison with even bicycle lamps. Full neck collars on horses are traditional in Western Europe and entirely functional but they are not intrinsically elegant and they do not enhance the beauty of a horse's neck and shoulders any more than a lavatory seat would enhance those of a beautiful woman if it were hung around her neck in the same position. Plaited manes are undeniably elegant and truly functional in that they enable unruly manes to be subdued and made tidy at short notice, but they are certainly not traditional for carriage horses. These considerations are valid for every aspect of the turnout of horses and carriages but many of them are covered by the specific requirements laid down for the judging of presentation so they need only be called to mind when any doubt exists.

The Driver and Groom(s)

The first requirement covers the clothes and the deportment of the driver, grooms and passenger. A single or tandem turnout may carry a passenger instead of a groom who, in this capacity, should remain seated in the cart, wearing a knee apron like the driver or a light rug, and not get out to attend to the horse except in emergency. Provided that the passenger is respectably dressed with an appropriate hat, and not smoking while the judge is looking, he or she can hardly be criticised or detract from the excellence of the turnout. A tandem needs a very well behaved leader if it is not to be attended by a groom, and a pair or four-in-hand must have one or two grooms respectively but need not carry a passenger as well, so that the latter is extraneous and should only be included if likely to add real lustre to the ensemble.

A gentleman driver should wear a bowler hat, a suit and black polished shoes, but may wear a black or grey top hat and a black, grey or fairly dark whole-coloured coat with a white stiff collar, an ordinary modern tie and black polished shoes if his grooms are in livery, and particularly if he drives a four-in-hand, despite his carriage being normally a sporting one. A lady driver should wear a close-fitting hat with a fairly narrow brim, a suit or dress with long sleeves, and low-heeled shoes. A driver of either sex must wear leather gloves.

While being inspected the driver must sit and hold the reins and whip as for driving but may reasonably rest his left hand on his knees after the judge has looked at him. The whip must be long enough, both in its stick and its thong, for the latter easily to reach the shoulders of the horses without the driver having to lean forward, and the thong of a whip for a pair should not be appreciably longer than that for a single horse or need to be caught up or held in any way. The thong of a team or tandem whip should be caught up and wound round the stick in the accepted manner (see illustration), and must not be tied or taped to the stick so as to be inoperable for use on the leaders.

Left: English bow-topped whips for pair or single. The whip reel keeps the top of the whip decent when not in use. Centre: English bow-topped team whip. Right: Hungarian thong team whip

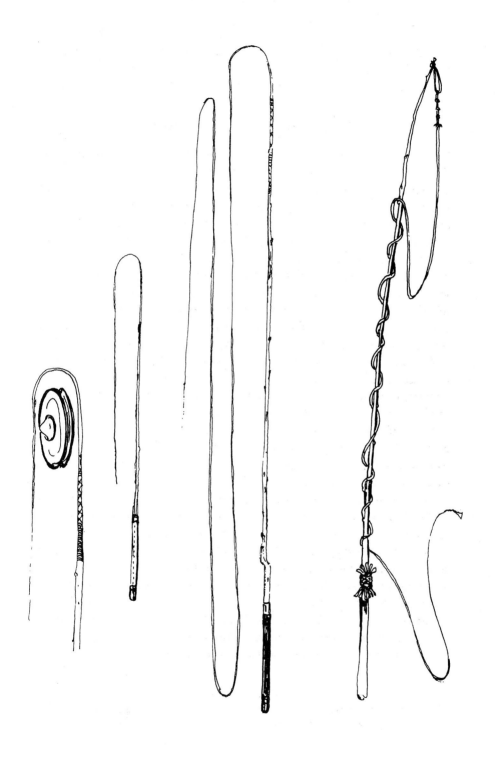

Grooms should stand in front of their horses, facing them; with a team, one of the two grooms should stand to the right of the wheelers. They need not hold the horses unless they need restraint but, if they do, should hold the bits or the cheek pieces of the bridles just above the bits, and not the reins.

Groom's livery in Western Europe is virtually a sealed pattern which, because it ceased to be functional, was not modified after the turn of the last century, and should not be altered from its original form. Top boots must be worn, without garter straps, and the tops may be brown or almost white 'champagne' ones but must match exactly for each groom of a four-in-hand. The white breeches may be slightly

Groom's collar and tie

cream coloured but should, ideally, not be very lightweight nylon ones. In the traditional pattern, breeches buttons were on the outside of the knee, and just below it, rather than on the inside, but this cut is long out of date and need no longer be insisted on.

The livery coat should hang to the mid-way point of the wearer's thigh. It may be black or of any essentially dark whole colour to complement the colours of the carriage. There should be six buttons down the front of the coat extending to the wearer's waist, but five only are permissible for very short grooms. There should be three pairs of buttons evenly spaced from the waist to the bottom of the coat down the skirts at the back of it. Buttons should be brass if the harness is brass mounted or silver if the harness mountings are white metal. They should carry a crest, badge or monogram, but the composition of the latter is unlikely to be investigated and a thrifty owner may save the considerable expense of having special ones made by using some of the less decipherable hunt, or even regimental, buttons. Esoteric variations in the cut and number of buttons of coats worn by people whose status in private service in the past was denoted by them are best ignored nowadays and both grooms with a four-in-hand should be dressed exactly alike.

A stiffly starched stand-up collar, without the wings which are appropriate with evening dress, should have a made-up 'Newmarket tie' fastened round it and the two folds of this should be fastened to the flap behind them with a small round-headed stick-pin. The pins should be the same for each of two grooms and the same coloured metal as the buttons. The heads of them may be in the form of small badges or ciphers. The collars may take some finding or contriving but the ties are sold in abundance to people who cannot tie their own hunting ones and these comparatively inexpensive components of a livery turnout are essential for a neat professional appearance.

Liveried carriage grooms must wear black top hats. British owners who hold a royal commission as an officer, serving or retired in the armed forces, or as a civil retainer of the Crown — and this is deemed by tacit consent to extend to Justices of the Peace — are entitled to fix cockades on their grooms' hats. Cockades are oval-shaped with fans for Army and Royal Air Force officers but without fans for Naval officers and civilians. Royal cockades are larger and circular with no fan and are strictly reserved for royal servants. Cockades incorporating colours are appropriate for owners who are citizens of some countries other than Britain. Cockades are by no means obligatory, so driving trials

Top, left to right: military and civil or naval cockades; below: royal cockade

competitors are advised to take advice from a better authority than a tailor or a hatter before making a hole in a hat; or to do without them.

Grooms in livery should wear brown leather gloves. These, together with the absence of garter straps, are an essentially functional tradition which should always be upheld.

Grooms may appropriately wear stable dress with any turnout in driving trials except when the driver is wearing a top hat when they should obviously not be dressed less formally than the master they are deemed to be serving. Correct stable dress for a man consists ideally of black polished shoes or ankle boots (not house shoes or slip-on shoes without laces), a dark grey or 'pepper-and-salt' tweed suit, a white stiff collar and black or soberly-patterned tie, a black bowler hat and brown leather gloves.

It is now generally conceded that girls acting as carriage grooms may wear full livery as if they were men. In this case they should be dressed exactly as their male counterparts and try to look as much like boys as possible, with their hair tucked well up underneath their top hats in a hair net.

There is no traditional justification for lady carriage grooms to be dressed in black butcher boots, white breeches, short black coats, hunting ties and hunting caps or bowler hats, and misogynists may declare that this order of dress is totally impractical for their task and often inelegant to boot. It has, however, come to stay and to be cherished as a convention by its practitioners, so that it must reasonably be regarded as synonymous with livery and judged by the same standards.

Stable dress for lady grooms is not yet bound to any tradition and can quite properly be dictated by their own good taste. Strong leather low-heeled shoes, and trousers, or at least jodhpurs, would seem to be a practical necessity and a coat rather than a blouse or a jersey does proper justice to the occasion. A more adventurous colour scheme than for men can be contemplated with blends or contrasts rather than exact matches, and this can be carried through to a bowler hat or hunting cap or even to a close-fitting neat felt hat. Like the men, women must wear brown leather gloves.

The rules prohibit grooms of either sex from wearing rugs or knee aprons or buttonholes and jewellery of any kind.

In Eastern Europe, except in Hungary, drivers and grooms all wear uniforms with breeches and boots and peaked caps, regardless of sex. These are not military uniforms, as many people suppose, but simply those of state employees like those of postmen and railwaymen in

One of Imre Abonyi's grooms at Lucerne, 1970, a Cziko from the Bugac
(Findlay Davidson)

Britain. They confer the advantage that judges cannot really criticise
them unless they are dirty.

The Hungarians are less state regimented than their fellow com-
munists but, with no top hat traditions, they dress their drivers in ordinary suits with soft felt hats and add a picturesque touch of pageantry

with the dress of their grooms. Depending on the stud from which the competitor is entered, the Hungarian grooms wear either the national costume of the Czikos, the famous horse herdsmen of the Puszta, or very colourful Hussar uniforms based on the liveries of noble Magyar families. The dress of the Czikos is still entirely genuine and varies only between the three Pusztas: the Bugac, the Mezohegyes and, the biggest and best known of them, the Hortobagy.

The Hussar uniforms have always been attractively Ruritanian, and in the early 1970s would have been an asset to any pantomime. They enraged the Hungarian magnates who had been deposed and exiled by the revolution, by copying and embellishing their hereditary liveries,

Light Hungarian harness, showing sallengs and pillongs

and reached their zenith in the person of an imposing dignitary who attended the European Championships at Windsor in 1973 as groom to one of the Hungarian competitors. For tassels and frogging he was a dead ringer for the Prisoner of Zenda and was, besides, startlingly accoutred with long spurs and a sword. In response to diffident enquiries about the purpose of this weapon, he said that it was for defence against bears and left his admirers baffled and slightly uneasy. The sobering influence of those who some regarded as spoil-sports prevailed, and the magnificence of this regalia was modified thereafter, but few judges still know what it really should be like and the dictates of diplomacy prevent them from expressing criticisms of it, or reflecting these in their marks.

Sandor Krizsan of Hungary in the presentation in the World Championships, 1984. His grooms are in Hussar dress, based on the old Magyar family liveries
(Findlay Davidson)

34

The Horses

The presentation rules confine the criteria by which the horses are to be judged to an assessment of their condition and turnout and an appreciation of whether those comprising teams, pairs or tandems are well matched or not. Good condition demands total cleanliness and a smooth coat with a fair bloom on it, although horses should not be expected to be as fat as they often, rather mistakenly, are in the show ring. They should be properly shod but this must be judged against an acceptable standard and not by a comparison of the apparent skill of one farrier against another. Evidence of incipient unsoundness, detectable by eye at the halt, can reasonably count against condition, as can serious blemishes, although continental judges seem to pay little regard to either of these. Conformation in itself is not a criterion, but conscientious judges can hardly be expected to rate as 'excellent' horses whose makes and shapes are obviously bad.

It is more important for driving trials horses to match in action and movement than in any other quality, but this cannot be judged at the halt in presentation so general build and type is the first consideration under this heading. To judge a team, or even a pair, in this respect

requires a view from above and behind the horses and not just from the front or the side where one always obscures the other. A difference in height of up to 5cm (2in) is relatively insignificant between leaders and wheelers in a team or tandem but is likely to keep a pair out of the top two ratings. Colour is the least important requirement for matching, but horses of different colours are not likely to be rated 'excellent' as a pair or team.

Assuming a good clean coat, turnout encompasses manes and tails and some trimming and tidying. A well-laid, unplaited carriage mane, not more than 15cm (6in) long, is every bit as good as a plaited one, and more traditionally correct. No part of any mane should be hogged or

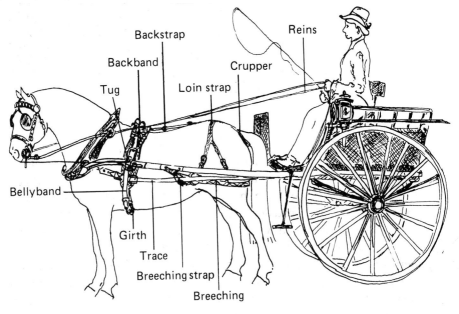

Single harness

clipped unless the whole of it has to be for a special reason; the long hairs and those lying underneath on the side to which it falls should be pulled — the task being done gradually over several weeks to prevent soreness. The tail should be only moderately pulled at the top from underneath in the same fashion and should hang to the point of the horse's hocks when he is moving and holding it normally with a crupper under it.

Fetlocks usually need tidying up but the clippers should be kept well away from them. Judicious pulling with some resin on the fingers will

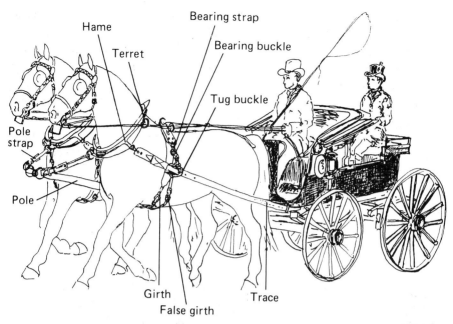

Hame

Terret

Bearing strap

Bearing buckle

Pole strap

Tug buckle

Pole

Girth

False girth

Trace

Pair harness with full or neck collars

often suffice, but scissors with a comb may need to be used in the same way that a barber cuts a man's hair. It is wrong to clip the whiskers from horses' muzzles; they use them to feel with and look no better without them. Hair which protrudes beyond the line of the edges of a horse's ears may be clipped or cut with scissors, but no hair should be removed from inside the ears. Feet may be well washed but should not be sandpapered. Clear hoof oil does them good and makes them look good, and harness blacking or boot polish can be applied to black hooves or black sections of them, but they should not be painted or lacquered under any circumstances.

The Harness

It is an axiom that harness must fit well and be properly adjusted, and if it does not or is not, to the extent of being liable to cause injury, pain or even discomfort to the horses which are wearing it, it can justifiably be rated as 'less than satisfactory' and probably 'less than sufficient'. The fitting of harness can be learned only by apprenticeship and not from a book, so it is not dealt with here.

Harness must seem, at least, to be a matching set, whether for a team,

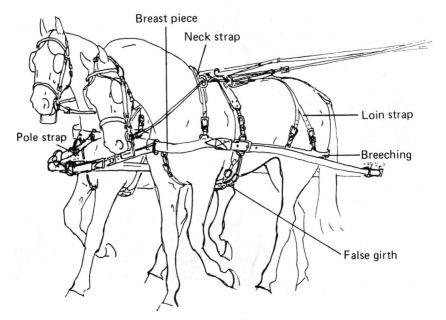

Pair harness with breast collars and breeching

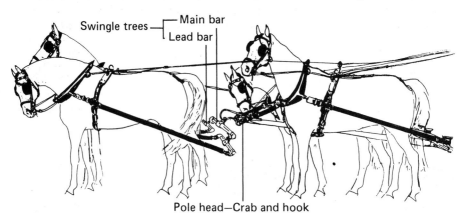

Team harness with full or neck collars

pair, tandem or single turnout, if it is to score 'good' or better. This means, in practice, buying a complete set to start with and ensuring that the widths and stitching of the leather and, more importantly, the shapes and designs of the buckles and other furniture are carefully matched for any repairs or alterations which have to be made.

To be worthy of being rated 'excellent', harness needs to be impressively well made, absolutely suitable for the types of horses and their

Quick release trace ends adapted by the Duke of Edinburgh from yachting. This fitting is particularly useful with marathon harness since it enables traces to be detached immediately in any accident situation *(Findlay Davidson)*

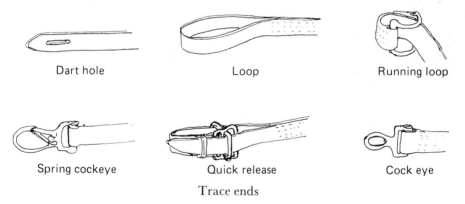

Dart hole	Loop	Running loop
Spring cockeye	Quick release	Cock eye

Trace ends

carriages, and put on without any faults, however trivial. Any extraneous straps, links or buckles should be removed, down to the lip strap links of curb chains; no strap shoud be fastened in the first or last hole since this suggests that it only just fits, and perhaps not quite perfectly; and buckles should be balanced on each side of each horse and lined up with one another, as on bridles, so as to suggest that the harness is made for the horse which wears it.

Jiri Kocman of Czechoslovakia presenting his Kladruber team at Windsor, 1975 *(Findlay Davidson)*

Brown harness is entirely suitable for use with varnished vehicles, but black harness always seems slightly more suitable with painted ones. Brass mountings seem to most people preferable to white metal ones.

Neck collars should not be preferred to breast collars although they tend to be in England. Tandem leaders can properly wear breast collars when the wheelers wear neck ones and there is an established precedent for this difference between the leaders and wheelers of a sporting team.

In Eastern Europe, Czechoslovakian harness is of English pattern and Poles drive with English-type harness but always with breast collars. Hungarian harness is fascinatingly different from almost any

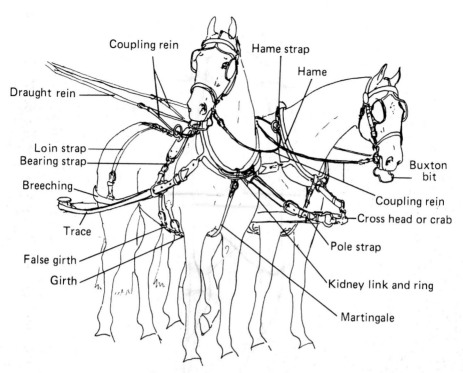

Coupling rein

Hame strap

Hame

Draught rein

Loin strap
Bearing strap

Breeching

Trace

False girth

Girth

Buxton
bit

Coupling rein

Cross head or crab

Pole strap

Kidney link and ring

Martingale

Pair harness with full collars

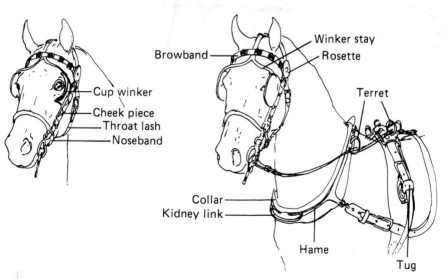

Browband

Winker stay

Rosette

Cup winker

Cheek piece

Throat lash

Noseband

Terret

Collar

Kidney link

Hame

Tug

Bridles: the cup winkers in the left-hand illustration are particularly appropriate for driving trials, since they give the horse a wider field of vision

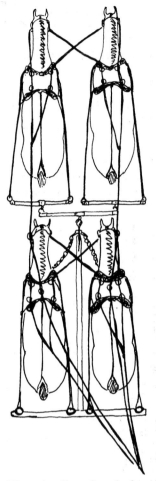

The reins for a four-in-hand

other and those who wish to study it academically should read Major Tibor Pettkó-Szandtner von Felsodriethoma's book *The Hungarian Driving Style* which is now available in an English translation.

The Vehicles

Carriages and carts must be completely sound and clean, and fit their horses as to the length and height of poles and shafts, and the width between the latter, to justify a rating of 'satisfactory' or better. To be in the 'good' bracket they must be entirely free from rust, with any apparent damage, including that to paintwork, expertly repaired, all their own proportions should be correct in relation to each other, the lamps and reflectors should be of suitable size and type and in working order, and the spare harness and equipment should be complete and neatly displayed.

'Excellent' should be reserved for a vehicle which, in addition, looks undeniably impressive as to its lines and colour scheme, including the seat cushions. Its bright metal fittings, other than the crab and those on the bars, will match the harness mountings, as will the polished parts of the lamps, and it will probably have a rear lamp as well as reflectors. The spare harness will be neatly stowed and immediately ready to hand and judges may be subconsciously impressed by the inclusion of extra equipment which, though not required by the rules, is likely to be more often needed, such as spare shoes and first aid boxes. The whole vehicle will present a distinctly glossy appearance as evidence of regular varnishing and frequent washing.

The General Impression

The general impression will be that which the judge gets of the harmony of proportions, lines and colour scheme of the whole turnout including the driver and his grooms and/or passenger. The suitability of the vehicle for the horses may enter into this, although a park carriage should never be preferred to a sporting one, and its height in relation to them will be significant. Very high vehicles are really out of place in driving trials but with a conventional English or Western European turnout the rein rail, or the top of the dashboard in its absence, should be no lower than the horses' croups. A two-wheeled cart should, of course, be quite level and not tilting forwards or backwards.

The driver should be seen to be sitting comfortably with his knees only slightly bent and his hips and the small of his back not above the sides of the vehicle or the back rest. Large people in small carts may be at an inevitably sad disadvantage in this respect.

It takes about eight tedious man hours to prepare a four-horse turnout for presentation, even when it all arrives at the event quite clean and in good order, and a single turnout will take at least three if it is to be worthily presented. The trouble which competitors take to produce these sparklingly impressive turnouts when they have many other matters to see to, and on occasions which for most of them are holidays from their normal work, is greatly appreciated by everyone who is associated with driving trials and must never be underrated or taken for granted.

3

Dressage

'He seems just to float along, doesn't he?'

Designated Competition AII, the dressage test is to judge the freedom, regularity of paces, harmony, lightness, ease of movement, impulsion and correct positioning of the horses. Competitors will also be judged on their style of driving, accuracy and general command of their horses. It is the counterpart of that in ridden horse trials although it necessarily takes place in a bigger arena.

The arena for teams and tandems is 100x40m and that for pairs and singles is normally 80x40m. The use of the smaller arena saves time as well as space and is customary at British events, though not obligatory. The marker letters are set out as for ridden dressage.

The limited number of possible movements for driven dressage is probably the main reason for the comparatively few tests which have been composed during the sixteen years since driving trials in their present form first started. Only four have been written to date for international rules, though there are two extra ones in the national rule book of the British Horse Society Driving Trials Group and the British Driving Society recognises a further one written specially for it by Sallie Walrond.

The most sophisticated of all these tests, and by far the most popular, is the alternative advanced test No 3. It has been prescribed for at least eighty per cent of all international and national trials, including the last three World Championships, and was composed by Colonel Donald Thackeray, the American Chairman of the International Driving Trials Committee, in 1978. It incorporates all, and more, of the figures and movements in the other tests, so it will serve well to illustrate all the requirements which dressage drivers have had to meet to date, and probably most of those which they may expect to encounter in future.

Timed to take ten minutes in the 100x40m arena or eight minutes in the 80x40m one it takes rather longer than trials organisers really like now, having regard to the increasing number of entries for which they are trying to cater.

Judges and Scoring

The jury normally consists of three judges with the president sitting at C and the other two at B and E respectively, but in important championships for teams of four horses there may be five judges sitting at C, M, F, K and H. This arrangement ensures that the whole arena is under close surveillance, though inevitably from slightly different points of view. An odd number of judges is desirable so that any whose scores are not orthodox may easily be detected if there is marked inconsistency between them.

As in ridden dressage, the president of the jury only is responsible for recording errors of course, and he must stop the competitor and tell him where he went wrong. Penalties for errors of course, or for grooms or passengers dismounting during the test are cumulative with 5 for the first incident, 10 for the second, 15 for the third and elimination for the fourth. The president of the jury must also stop the test and eliminate the competitor if he considers that any horse involved is markedly lame. The other judges are not concerned with this decision, against which there can be no appeal.

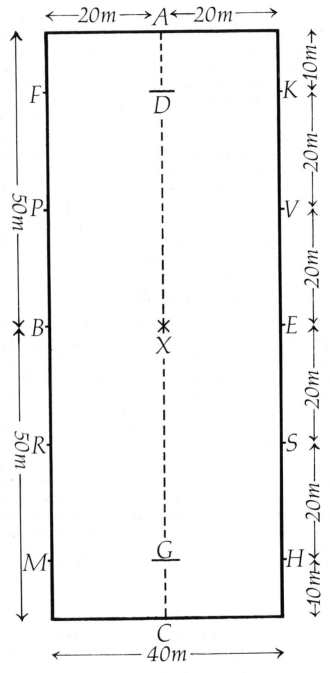

Diagram of a full-size dressage arena

Driven dressage tests are no longer timed for purposes of penalising those who take too long since this procedure, which was in force until 1984, was not relevant to the execution of the tests and sometimes added undue penalties when a competitor had to correct an error of course made during a long movement.

The format of eleven specific movements and four general assessments each to be graded out of a total of 10 marks makes a possible total of 150 good marks for the test, and these are divided by the number of judges involved so as to produce an average, which is converted to penalty points by being subtracted from 150. All tests so far, regardless of the time they are expected to take, have comprised eleven movements as well as the four general assessments, and there is enough flexibility for this format to be retained in any test whether it is timed for five or ten minutes, so that the scoring and thus the relative influence of the dressage competition will remain constant.

The Dressage Movements

Movements in driven dressage are inevitably limited in comparison with those which are possible in a ridden test, because of the restrictions imposed by the vehicle. The collected and extended trot, as well as the working trot, is always asked for, but only a good extended walk with light rein contact is expected or required. The rein back is always a requirement and often a critical one as regards the scoring, but until 1986 no movement at the canter was prescribed for any driven dressage test.

A new test for 1986 may, however, incorporate some work at the canter and this, though unconventional for carriage horses, will add a touch of sporting spectacle to this otherwise rather sedate competition. It is not unheard of, or even totally untraditional, for horses to gallop in team or pair harness, although the motion transmitted through the shafts may be found to have an unsettling effect on the occupants of single and tandem carts and will certainly not enhance their dignity.

The Walk

The walk required for driven tests is, in effect, an extended one with the hind feet coming to the ground in front of the footprints of the forefeet to display a clear 'over track'.

Current tests require that horses should walk 'on the bit', but a very

F.E.I. DRESSAGE TEST No.3 ALTERNATIVE ADVANCED 1978

(As amended 1980)

Competitor's No. ....

Time: 10 minutes

MOVEMENT		TO BE JUDGED	Mark 0 - 10	REMARKS
1. A X X	Enter collected trot Halt, salute Working trot	Driving in on a straight line standing on the bit, trans, to halt and to working trot.		
2. XGMB BX XM	Working trot ½ circle to right (20m) Return to track at M	Impulsion, regularity and accuracy of figures.		
3. MCHE EX XH HCM	Working trot ½ circle to left (20m) Return to track at H Working trot	Impulsion, regularity and accuracy of figures.		
		Transition to extended trot		
4. MXK K	Extended trot Collected trot	Extension, regularity transition to collected trot		
5. KAF	Circle at A (30m) left reins in one hand. On completion of circle, reins at discretion	Accuracy of figure Regularity		
		Transition to extended trot		
6. FXH H	Extended trot Collected trot	Extension, regularity Transition to collected trot		
7. HCM M	Circle at (30m) right reins in one hand, on completion of circle reins at discretion Working trot	Accuracy of figures Regularity Transition to working trot		
8. MSBV -FDX X	Serpentine of 5 loops (20m diam) each turn Walk on bit	Accuracy of figures Regularity Transition to walk		
9. XG G	Walk Halt 10 sec immobility Rein back 3m Walk	Straightness, impulsion regularity Transition to halt Immobility, straightness Transition to rein back and walk		
10. GMXK K	Walk Collected trot	Impulsion, regularity Transition to collected trot		
11. KDKD DFD DG G	Circle to left at D followed immediately by circle right (20m) Extended trot Halt, salute	Accuracy of figure, regularity transition to extended trot Extension straightness Transition to halt, standing on the bit		
	Leave arena at trot	Regularity and freedom (if team maintenance of pace by all horses)		
12.	Paces			
13.	Impulsion	Moving forward (if team all horses working)		
14.	Obedience, lightness	Response to aids, willing and without resistance		
15.	Driver	Use of aids, handling of reins and whip Position on box. Accuracy of figures		

10. Excellent
9. Very Good
8. Good
7. Fairly Good
6. Satisfactory

5. Sufficient
4. Insufficient
3. Fairly Bad
2. Bad
1. Very Bad
0. Not performed

Signature of Judge .... Total ....

TO BE MARKED ON THE PRESIDENT OF THE JURY'S JUDGING SHEET ONLY

for errors of course and dismounting of grooms

First incident	5 penalty points
Second incident	10 penalty points
Third incident	15 penalty points
Fourth incident	Elimination

Exceeding the Time Allowed (0.5 penalty points per commenced second)

Time taken for test   seconds
Time Allowed   seconds
Time exceeding Time Allowed   seconds
Penalty Points
(Time exceeding Time Allowed x 0.5 seconds)

Signature of President of the Jury ....

1982 Edition

I.P.H.

FEI Dressage Test No 3 Alternative Advanced 1978

light rein contact only is required and, provided that the reins are not noticeably slack, most horses will walk best in harness if their heads and necks are free and unrestricted by the reins. If the arena is level, the ground is not too hard and the grass is three or four inches long, the carriage wheels will meet enough resistance for the wheelers of a team or tandem to be in draught throughout any walk movement, but the leaders should only 'carry their bars' and not be fully in draught to an extent which might upset the regularity of the wheelers' paces.

The natural movement of a horse's head and neck when it is walking normally, added to the effective difference in the length of the reins when it is pulling the cart forward as opposed to holding it back, makes it virtually impossible for a driver to maintain *firm*, even contact with his horses' mouths at the walk, particularly in the case of a four-in-hand. These considerations would frustrate any attempt to achieve a collected walk which would result in horses pulling their carts largely on their mouths. This pace is not therefore demanded in any current tests and its incorporation in any future ones would be undesirable. A free walk on a loose rein is perfectly feasible for harness horses, and demonstrates their willingness to relax and display a calm, happy temperament and state of mind. It should be instantly attainable and figure prominently in all schooling sessions, but the time factor may continue to exclude it from any actual tests.

Regularity is an essential prerequisite for the walk as for all other paces. The four legs of the horse must follow one another in coming to the ground in an exactly regular four-time sequence in which the near-fore follows the near-hind and is followed by the off-hind and off-fore. The length of the step, which is that between the imprints of the two forefeet, should be equal throughout the movement and the imprints of the hind feet should be in front of those of the forefeet by exactly equal lengths. The horse must walk straight forward to the appropriate marker with energy and determination, since any wavering from the straight line is likely to interrupt his rhythm as well as to give an impression of hesitancy or loss of impulsion.

Because they can rely on only limited guidance from the reins at the walk, it is fortunate that most well-schooled horses seem to be able to identify the correct markers and are normally most co-operative in marching resolutely to them and ignoring the many distractions which usually surround them.

The Trot

The following paragraphs about the trot in driven dressage are reprinted by kind permission of the editors of the Swiss magazine *Achenbach* to which I contributed them in 1984. They are comprehensive to the point of being partly of academic rather than practical interest, but most of the information in them is relevant to the driving of dressage tests and the necessary schooling for them.

The trot is a gait in two-time in which the paired diagonal feet strike and leave the ground simultaneously with a brief period of suspension between each beat; and nearly all horsemen know this instinctively but seldom think about it very much. The essential difference between the three different trots is in the length of the stride involved. The stride, properly speaking, is the distance between successive imprints of the same feet, as opposed to the step which is the distance between imprints of the two forefeet or two hind feet. In extended trot the horse's stride will be about twice as long as it should be in collected trot, and in working trot its length will be approximately between the two.

All three trots, and of course the walk, must be absolutely regular both as to length of step and as to rhythm. A sound horse with good feet in its natural state will normally step regularly, but incorrect riding, driving or even shoeing, as well as any hint of lameness, may interfere with this natural regularity and, if such cause is prolonged, irregularity may persist even without the original reason for it, and will be very difficult to put right. A horse which steps irregularly will normally do so at all paces, so it is wise, and easiest, to examine the walk of any intended purchase very carefully, even to the extent of measuring the length of its steps as imprinted on a straight sand track. A horse which steps regularly may be induced to become irregular in its step by being lunged or worked in a small circle on one rein much more than on the other, by its rider sitting down much more on one diagonal than the other at the trot, or by its being ridden or driven in such a manner that its head is not straight and it becomes one sided.

Rhythm is the tempo or cadence of the hoof beats and this should be regular for each stride and for all strides of the duration of the trot throughout a movement. In addition, it should remain constant for all movements at the trot throughout the test regardless of whether the horse is required to demonstrate collected, working or extended trot. Of course, if the step itself is not regular the rhythm is not likely to be absolutely regular either. Regularity is one of the stated requirements to be judged in almost all the movements of the current dressage tests. In accordance with the accepted conventions of dressage judging, a judge should not award more than 6 marks if he finds one of these stated requirements to be noticeably lacking, so that regularity is of prime importance and without it a test is never likely to be more than satisfactory.

The most common fault is for the tempo to quicken in extended trot. This spoils the movement even when a degree of extension is achieved, and may lead to the criticism that the horse is 'running' rather than extending its stride. The tempo may also quicken inadvertently just after the horse has completed a circle and has straightened to trot in the track of the arena. Drivers should guard against this tendency by maintaining firm contact through the reins and not giving way to a moment of relaxation.

There is a natural tendency for the tempo to become slower in collected trot. This is a less serious fault than that it should quicken in extension, and many judges may not notice it provided that the rhythm is not interrupted and the cadence remains regular. However, any loss of impulsion or tendency to be behind the bit will usually interrupt the rhythm and may result in variations of pace.

The tempo of the trot will understandably vary between different horses; it will be quicker for small ponies than for big horses. The best tempo for the horse concerned will probably be that which comes naturally to him at a fairly relaxed working trot with quite light rein contact. Some drivers, and some judges, do not have a natural sense of rhythm; one might even conceive of their having to resort to a metronome to judge accurately the regularity of a horse's paces. It has been suggested that music played in absolutely strict tempo to suit the cadence of the horse's paces may help him to maintain a regular rhythm at the trot.

Propulsion for the trot, as for all other paces, must come from the hind legs, and good judges will usually watch these more closely than the front ones to make sure that the hocks are being engaged strongly and actively well underneath the horse and not just trailing along behind it. A horse which does not use his hocks properly is likely to be heavy on the forehand and to seem to be sloping downwards from his croup to his withers rather than upwards, which is desirable. His action will probably seem to be ponderous and plodding rather than light and active. His head carriage may well be too low. He is likely to be generally heavy on the hand and he may eventually seek to evade the bit by tucking his chin into his chest and becoming 'over bent'.

The ideal centre of balance for harness horses pulling light carriages is probably slightly further back than that for ridden horses, but it takes time to achieve this exactly and young or unfit horses cannot be expected to display an ideal outline in this respect.

A horse which is regularly required to pull a heavy load, ie one heavier than his own weight or even one approximating to it through heavy going, must necessarily use his weight rather than the power of his hind legs alone to start the carriage and, from time to time, to keep it moving. He will need to lean forward to do this and will inevitably become too much 'on his forehand'. This fault is much more difficult to eradicate than the opposite one in which a horse carries his head too high and tends to 'stargaze' and be 'above the bit'.

The ideal head carriage for a harness horse is slightly higher than that for a ridden one and he should show a more pronounced bend at the poll; this bend must in no circumstances be further back down the neck. At risk of seeming heretical, I believe that a very limited variation in head carriage is permissible between horses of different conformations and even different breeds. Some will appear at their best when they seem to be held well together with the line of their faces vertical to the ground, while others will present a more pleasing appearance if their necks and heads are a little more elongated. In collected

British National Champion Jill Neill driving her Welsh Mountain pony Coed Coch Pippin at Sandringham in 1984. This shows a good extended trot *(Leslie Lane)*

trot, the line of the face of most horses should be vertical to the ground, though not ever making an acute angle with it. In working trot the head may be slightly lowered and the nose fractionally advanced, and in extended trot the nose may reasonably be advanced a little further still. It is said that moving horses cannot put their forefeet on the ground at any point beyond that directly below their noses. This is clearly not true for a well-balanced horse in extended trot, as can be demonstrated in the case of most good Hackneys who invariably display spectacular extension without any noticeable straightening of their necks and heads.

Much the best way to teach a horse to develop a good extended trot is to ride him. A competent rider with a firm independent seat and sympathetic hands is required, though he need not be an expert dressage rider. The rider should give a clear unmistakable voice command at the same time that he uses his legs and back to induce the extended trot, so that the necessary association of ideas will be established, and it may be helpful to hiss in rhythm with the step, at least for the first few strides. A separate command should be used for collected trot and a click in rhythm with the step instead of a hiss will help to establish the correct cadence.

A horse may be taught the collected trot in long reins and worked success-fully in it, but the operator must be fairly expert at long reining since otherwise more harm than good will result.

To be able to do good dressage tests in harness, a horse must be ridden fairly frequently, for anything up to half the total time of his work. A number of drivers who cannot ride themselves or get other people to ride their horses for them seem to manage well without this facility, but without occasional correction and encouragement from a rider, it is difficult to achieve a good extended trot and the collected trot will often seem to lack impulsion as well as the cadence which seems to be associated with an elevated step.

52

Claudia Bunn driving her Welsh Mountain pony team at Brighton in 1983. She is doing a circle with reins in one hand *(K. G. Ettridge, Horse & Driving)*

Turns and Circles

Circles and half circles of less than 20m in diameter have not yet been demanded in any driven dressage test and, although 10m circles could be described quite easily, the inevitable loss of rhythm entailed would interrupt the flow of the test and make them undesirable from an aesthetic point of view.

Pairs and singles could drive a circle of only 10m diameter without losing the rhythm or regularity of their pace at the trot, and may conceivably be asked to do so in the future, but tandems and even more so teams need a turning circle of this size if they are to maintain their pace even at the collected trot.

Right angle turns of 90 degrees, taken at the trot in the corners of the arena or onto or from the centre line, are in effect quarter circles of about 10m diameter for teams and tandems as well as pairs and singles, although a tighter turn than this can be achieved at the walk without any interruption of the pace. The need to maintain the pace and stay within the boards must be balanced against the desirability of keeping in the track and not cutting the corners.

Ideally, horses' heads should be bent slightly inwards towards the direction of the turn. They should certainly not be bent outwards away from it, but there can be no criticism if harness horses' heads remain straight during turns and circles, and it can be assumed that they are looking inwards with their eyes. It is a great mistake to attempt to

Tandem turnout: breast collar on leader, neck collar on wheeler. A conventional method

correct any 'falling in' on the circle by tightening the outside rein(s) because this will inevitably aggravate the problem and cause the horses' heads to be bent outwards.

The achievement of a correct bend, slightly inwards, or at least the avoidance of an incorrect outward bend, is a matter of delicately precise rein handling. The technique involves indicating the direction of the turn by a tweak on the inside rein at exactly the right moment and thereafter giving with the outside rein rather than taking with the inside one. Provided the tension on the inside rein remains even and constant

HRH The Duke of Edinburgh in the World Championships in Holland in 1982. This demonstrates the correct positioning between leaders and wheelers during a turn so as to form the necessary hinge *(Findlay Davidson)*

the horse will reach forward imperceptibly to maintain contact with the outside one and turn his head slightly inwards in the process.

An attempt to induce the turn simply by increasing tension on the inside rein will cause the horse to alter course quite effectively but he will almost immediately begin to resist the stronger contact on one side of his mouth and bend his head outwards accordingly, thereby advancing his inside shoulder and starting to cut or 'fall in' on the circle. The procedure may be likened to that which would be employed if the reins were rigid steel rods or elongated bicycle handles when the turn would be made by pushing with the outside hand rather than pulling with the inside one.

This same technique is employed in ridden dressage and all correct school riding but it is more difficult to perfect with driven horses owing to the greater length of the reins and the need to make much bigger adjustments between extension in draught and collection with the vehicle being held back by breeching or pole straps. The procedure is further complicated when two or four horses are involved although a pair or the leaders of a team can be treated, in effect, as a single horse during turns and circles as the coupling reins should be adjusted to compensate for differences between them.

The principle of giving with the outside rein rather than taking with the inside one is crucial to the proper execution of turns and circles in dressage. Sadly, it may be true that about one person in six will never acquire the muscular co-ordination and sympathetic reaction speed to execute this technique satisfactorily.

There is, in effect, a hinge between the leaders and wheelers of a team or tandem which enables them to make turns and circles without cutting corners. When a team is describing a 20m right-hand circle the horses should be so positioned in relation to each other that the nose of the off-wheeler is between the quarters of the two leaders, and the near-wheeler's nose occupies the same position for left-hand circles. Unless this positioning is maintained the circle is likely to be inaccurate.

The Rein Back

A dressage test may be won or lost on the strength of the rein back, since if it is very crooked or does not cover the required 3m it may well be rated as 'insufficient', for a loss of a possible 6 marks. It is extremely difficult to rein back straight from a crooked halt, even with a single horse driven to a two-wheeled vehicle, and almost impossible to do this with a pair or team driven to a four-wheeled one. It is therefore essential to halt with the wheels exactly parallel with the centre line and this requirement may have to be balanced against the need to halt with the horses' forefeet exactly on the mark. If both these requirements cannot be achieved the latter may be rather less important than the former.

Even from a dead square halt the rein back can still be crooked if the horses display any resistance to or evasion from the increased rein contact by which, coupled with a voice command, the movement must be initiated. It is possible to straighten out a curve, even within the 3m, with a two-wheeled vehicle but very difficult with a four-wheeled one, particularly if the horses are not moving back together. A device for temporarily locking the forecarriage, which was contemplated by many drivers for several years and would have been most helpful in the rein back, was forbidden by the rules in 1983 before anyone could get round to constructing it.

The concept of setting up impulsion and restraining it so that reverse movement is induced, which is valid in ridden dressage, is not practicable for horses in harness, so ready obedience to the driver's voice and an unresisting response to increased and even pressure from the reins are the keys to a good rein back. With teams or tandems the best technique is to take up the contact only on the wheel reins and allow the leaders to be drawn back automatically by the lead reins, whose length should remain unadjusted.

Lateral Movements and Flexion

Because horses have a shaft on each side of them in single harness and must remain parallel to the pole in pair harness, they cannot attempt lateral movements or work on two tracks. George Bowman can in fact demonstrate a very passable shoulder-in with the leaders only of his team and, since this is achieved solely with reins and voice, it amounts to horsemanship of a very high order. Regrettably, it fails to impress spectators, most of whom conclude that the horses are just going crooked and, since it is of little practical significance, it is unlikely ever to be incorporated in an official driven test.

The rigidity imposed by poles and shafts and the absence of a rider's inside leg also inhibit the achievement of lateral flexions to a degree which a ridden dressage judge might like to see. It is much easier to prevent ridden horses from 'falling-in' on their circles than driven ones, and the latter will be more inclined to do this because they must push or pull slightly against the shafts or pole to steer the vehicle. Judicious use of the whip on single horses, pairs or wheelers can help to prevent horses 'falling in' or swinging their quarters out on circles, but at the risk of impaired rein contact since the right hand must be removed from the reins while the whip is applied.

New Movements and Innovations

The concept of driven dressage tests following quite closely the format of ridden ones is sensible and helps to standardise the judging of them. There are some movements and manoeuvres of particular significance to horses in harness which have not yet been asked for and which could increase the scope of future driven tests. A turn at right angles with leaders and wheelers being required to turn exactly on the mark rather than following round in a curve or half circle is very practical for harness horses, as when they have to turn through a gateway off a narrow lane. A swing through 90 or 180 degrees with the carriage remaining stationary is also likely to be called for in practice almost as often as a rein back.

The passage and even the piaffer can be demonstrated quite effectively in harness, particularly by a single horse or pony. However, the extra impulsion called for is difficult to set up without leg aids or a firm position on the ground close to the horse, and very hard to contain through the whole length of driving reins, particularly if four horses are involved. Indeed, most drivers find that the necessary rein contact with four horses is quite as strong as they care to cope with just at the collected trot, so these movements, although they would be spectacular, are not likely to be acceptable for driven dressage.

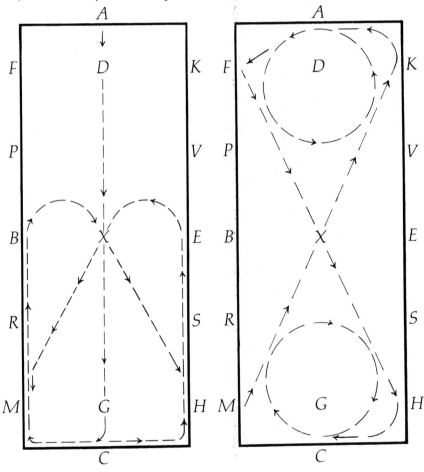

Learning Dressage Tests

As in ridden dressage, tests must be driven from memory, and people who are new to any form of equestrian school work are often anxious about remembering them. They are, however, generally simpler and easier to learn than ridden tests and the driver has an advantage over the rider in having a companion, groom or passenger, with him who must not give visible aid or indications but is not forbidden to talk and cannot be heard anyway if he does so quietly by way of a timely prompt.

The four patterns which make up Test No 3 Alternative Advanced. *Left to right:* the entry and 'pear drops'; the extended trots and one-handed circle; the serpentine and rein back; the walk and double circles

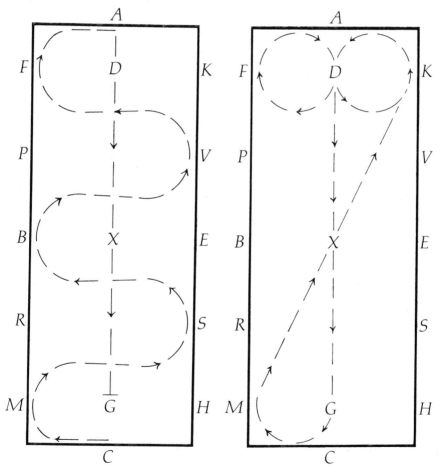

There is a simple technique for learning and remembering dressage tests which is so obvious to many people that they do not think of advising others about it. It consists in appreciating that all tests are composed of a number of basic patterns formed from logically linked movements. There are invariably far fewer patterns than movements which comprise them, and they are, in themselves, relatively easy to learn and remember, provided that they are visualised as complete patterns and not traced as a track from one letter around the arena to the next. There is a risk of forgetting the sequence of patterns or which one comes next, but the groom or passenger can give a reminder about this provided that a name for each pattern has been agreed. He can also warn discreetly when the pace is not correct: usually working trot instead of collected trot or vice versa.

Driving Styles

Any method or style of driving is permitted by the rules in dressage as in the other competitions of driving trials. The true two-handed Hungarian style, in which both hands are held over the reins with their backs facing upward and the coupling buckles of the lead and wheel reins are very precisely adjusted just in front of the driver's fingers, is entirely effective in the hands of those who are well practised in it, but the English or Achenbach style seems to provide for more precise and

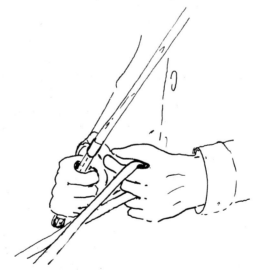

English or Achenbach rein handling for pair or single

Pedro Arpad of Spain driving his Andalucian team at the European Championships in Switzerland, 1981. This is traditional Spanish turnout *(Leslie Lane)*

flexible adjustment between lead and wheel for tandem drivers and four-horse coachmen who have learned this method.

The degree of impulsion which harness horses need to display to perform a strong, lively dressage test, and the length, friction and actual weight of the reins by which this is controlled, results in a tension on the driver's hand equivalent to a weight of not less than 4lb for each horse involved. With a team of four horses, this weight can make considerable physical demands on the coachman and, if one of the horses is a puller, particularly one of the leaders, the strain on the driver's hand, wrist and forearm can become almost unbearable. Some well-known coachmen have had to retire in the middle of dressage tests for this reason, and George Bowman nearly found himself in this embarrassing position in the World Championships in Holland in 1982.

A conventional method of holding the reins offers the best way of combating the strain involved and avoiding the risk of muscular cramp. This can be learned properly only from a teacher and supervised practice, though illustrations can show the principles involved and a student can learn a great deal by sitting beside a good coachman provided that he watches the driver's hands and not the horses.

Correct rein handling technique is crucial to the proper execution of the English or Achenbach style of driving. The four reins must never leave the coachman's left hand and the right hand normally remains in front of it also holding all four reins and the whip. The right hand must

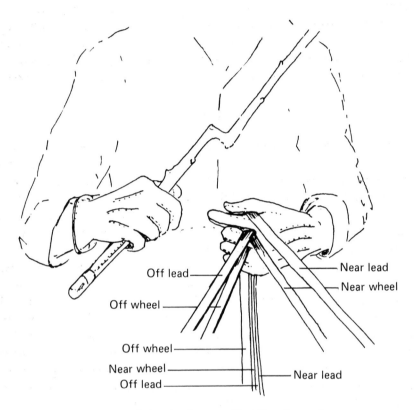

Off lead

Off wheel

Off wheel

Near wheel

Off lead

Near lead

Near wheel

Near lead

English or Achenbach way of holding four reins

be removed from the reins to use the whip and must also act independently from the left to take up any rein and shorten it or loop it under the left thumb when turns are to be made. It must also be ready to shorten any one or two or all four reins by pulling them through the fingers of the left hand from behind it.

A good coachman must be able to take up any one or two reins with his right hand instantly and instinctively without taking his eyes off his leaders or the pole head between his wheelers if he is to be confident of making precise, accurate turns.

The Voice

The use of the driver's voice is entirely permissible in driven dressage since it takes the place of the rider's legs, back and adjusted body weight in calling for forward movement and inducing impulsion. Nervous horses can be calmed by soothing conversation addressed to them, but this is inappropriate and confusing in a dressage test and only clear specific commands should be given. Harness horses must always know their own names and react instantly to them so that it is wrong to change them or to use stable names and stud names indiscriminately.

Matching the Paces

The need for horses in pair and team harness to move together and step equally is an essential requirement for a good dressage test and the successful achievement of it marks a pinnacle in the progress of an ambitious trials driver. It is difficult and often expensive to acquire a pair of horses whose natural paces match exactly, and even more so to find a perfectly matched team. Exact similarity in size and shape is not, however, crucial to the achievement of this aim.

Provided that their conformation is comparable, horses can match well in their paces even if there is a difference of up to 5cm (2in) in their respective heights. The horse which moves less freely in a pair will almost always make strenuous efforts to match the stride of his better-moving partner, who becomes the dominant one in this respect. The same provision applies to only a slightly lesser extent between leaders and wheelers in a team, and it is fortunate that the opposite procedure hardly ever prevails so that there is little risk of the better mover restricting his stride to match that of the less good one.

Dressage to Music

In 1980, the organisers of Lowther Driving Trials followed the lead given by Lord March at his ridden dressage championships at Goodwood in staging a free dressage test, or *Kür*, to music for drivers. There have been no other free dressage tests to music driven in public in England and since driven dressage has only taken place in conjunction with complete driving trials, in which programme time is at a premium, the growth of this innovation is not likely to be rapid. However, the concept of a competition in which drivers compose their own tests, incorporating novelty and ingenuity beyond the scope of the standard ones, and select their own music to accompany them, has obvious attractions, particularly for spectators for whom the stereotyped repetition of the official tests is undeniably tedious.

Free tests, which are performed more frequently on the continent than in Britain, are prescribed in the international driving trials rules to be arranged separately from the combined event and to be judged for general impression as well as content. There is no prohibition on judges displaying their marks at the end of each test to add to spectator interest.

The provision of special taped music for dressage tests is now becoming a semi-professional study in itself. There is available plenty of good music in strict trot tempo and recent technology has produced a sophisticated amplifying system which enables its speed to be varied without any effect on its pitch or tone.

Driven dressage is probably too circumscribed to become a separate equestrian activity meriting shows or events devoted solely to it, so we cannot anticipate many free dressage tests being added to the already crowded timetables of driving trials. It may, however, be not entirely inconceivable in the foreseeable future to contemplate the possibility of free tests to music replacing the existing standard ones for Competition AII of trials and thereby increasing their appeal to spectators and the artistic ingenuity demanded of competitors.

4
The Marathon

'I'm sure it's not as heavy as it was when we started.'

The name 'marathon' for Competition B of a driving trial is a misnomer because Pheidippides who in 490BC raced from Marathon to Athens bearing news of a Greek victory over the Persians and established the name to signify an athletic endeavour, covered the distance of 26 miles on his feet and not in any sort of a horse and cart. His run was a considerable feat of endurance, as have been all the foot races competed for over a similar distance ever since, but the 27km (17 miles) maximum which horses cover in driving trials, with two compulsory ten-minute halts and two separate kilometres during which they must walk, is at most just a reasonable test of stamina and less strenuous for them than a good day's hunting.

Distance and Speeds

The object of the marathon, as declared in the international rules, is to test the standard of fitness and stamina of the horses and the judgement of pace and horsemastership of the competitor. A full marathon of five sections is about 27km long and consists of two sections each 10km long (Sections A and E) to be driven at the trot at a speed of 15kph (9mph), one section 5km long (Section C) to be driven at a fast trot of 20kph (12½mph), and two sections each about 1,200 long (Sections B and D) to be driven at the walk at a speed of 7kph (4¼mph). The end of each kilometre in Sections A and E is indicated by a marker at the side of the track.

At the end of each walk section there is a compulsory halt of ten minutes during which horses are inspected by a judge to ensure that they are fit to continue. There is always a vet at the second of these halts to advise the judge about the fitness of horses and, at big events, there is often a vet at the first halt as well.

For ponies, the speed of the fast trotting section (Section C) is reduced by 2kph to 18kph (11¼mph), and the speed of each walk section is reduced by 1kph to 6kph (3¾mph). The speeds laid down are maximum ones and may be reduced by the technical delegate to take account of very difficult going. In exceptional circumstances the

British National Champion Lyn Bourn driving John Ravenscroft's Hackney Sunbeam Bomber at Sandringham 1984 *(Sandra M. Caton, Horse & Driving)*

ground jury may also reduce the speeds after the jury president has had the arrangements handed over to him by the technical delegate.

Natural hazards such as water crossings and narrow gateways are invariably incorporated in all three trotting sections, though not in the walk sections which should be on good going over level ground. There must also be specially-constructed obstacles in Section E, not less than five in number and not more than eight, and they must be not less than 200m apart and built in accordance with laid down rules. Since these obstacles constitute the main means by which competitors are awarded penalties in a marathon, and thus dominate the scoring of it, it is customary to have the full eight, or at least seven of them.

The number of sections in a marathon may be reduced to suit the timetable of an event which does not last for three days. A one-day event may well have a marathon of only one section, in which case it will include the special obstacles and, by tacit agreement in British trials though not officially sanctioned by the rules, this one section may be more than 10km in length. A one-day event may have a three-section marathon (Sections A, B and E) and a two-day event may have a three-section or a full five-section course. If a marathon is shortened in this way to fit a timetable, or a restricted area of land, there must be a walk section and a compulsory halt between two trotting sections and the lengths of the sections should comply with the rules. There is no point in having a walk section to follow a single trotting section to finish a marathon, nor in starting a marathon with a walk section.

Time Penalties

The time allowed for each section is calculated from the speed demanded for it, the distances being established so that the time allowed is in whole minutes. Competitors who take longer than the time allowed to complete any section are given 1 penalty point for every commenced period of 5 seconds by which they exceed it; so that 1 second over time allowed costs 1 penalty, and 6 seconds over costs 2 penalties etc. Because the timing equipment is more accurate than it has ever been before, a 1985 concession in the rules allows penalties to be recorded at the rate of 0.2 penalty points for each second over the time allowed for each section. Under current rules, competitors who finish Sections A or C in less than the minimum time prescribed, which is 2 minutes less than the maximum time allowed in Section A, and 1 minute less in Section C, are given half a penalty for each commenced period of 5 seconds by which they finish in less than the minimum time. Thus, if the time allowed is 40 minutes the minimum time will be 38 minutes for Section A and 39 minutes for Section C, so that a competitor who finishes Section A in 37 minutes 59 seconds will be given 0.5 penalties, and one who finishes it in 37 seconds 55 seconds will be given 1 penalty. No minimum time has ever been prescribed for the walk sections since they would obviously be quite unattainable.

The peculiar ruling which penalises competitors for driving faster than they need, though at the correct pace, stems from a curious misconception that the maintenance of a constant speed is an essential attribute of coachmanship. This misconception is still enshrined in the rules in the statement that the competition is primarily a test of regularity, and is emphasised by the rule that no speedometer may be fitted to a carriage as an artificial aid to achieving this. The marathon is not, of course, primarily a test of regularity and it would be very dull if it were. The idea probably stems from a misunderstanding about the need for mail coachmen during the nineteenth century to have been on time for each of their stages. With very tight timetables and less than two minutes allowed to change teams, it was almost impossible to make up lost time and delays would have been cumulative and resulted in bad timekeeping. No mail coachman would, however, have incurred rebuke for being early at a stage although he would seldom have been able to achieve this.

The idea that judgement of pace is demonstrated by maintaining a constant speed is also a misconception. As related to riding or driving horses, this is a matter of adjusting their speed according to the going and gradients so as to enable them to cover the required distance in the shortest time and, in races with other horses, usually to finish faster than their rivals. It is often necessary to moderate speeds to avoid horses becoming too tired to maintain their pace towards the end of a journey, but this is a matter of nursing them over difficult ground and husbanding their energy, not of keeping them to a constant speed.

In the early days of the ridden three-day event, competitors were penalised for finishing the roads and tracks sections earlier than required, but this rule was acknowledged to be irrelevant and abandoned many years ago. The same understanding will no doubt be arrived at as regards driving trials in the foreseeable future and the complete abandonment of minimum times and the confusion and complications with which they are associated will be welcomed by competitors, scorers and spectators alike.

Navigation

The idea that marathon sections must not be completed in less than a stated time is also responsible for a complicated concept in the minds of competitors which is identified, erroneously, as navigation. Those who are concerned to practise this — and the concern is confined almost exclusively to British drivers — take great trouble to note exactly which point of the route they have reached at any given time and increase or reduce their speed to try to reach prearranged markers in accordance with personal timetables which they have drawn up while making a reconnaisance of the course. This requires quite complicated calculations which tend to distract grooms from their essential task of helping their drivers to stay on the correct route. It is unnecessary, and occasionally disastrous when a miscalculation or the wrong identification of a marker results in an untimely reduction of speed.

In practice, drivers should allow their horses to trot on as fast as they want to in Section A, not pressing them in any way and only restraining them to avoid breaks of pace or risk of injury in bad going. They must, however, be able to identify with certainty the last kilometre marker in the section and must know the time accurately at this point so as to be able to reduce speed if necessary and finish the section within the generous bracket of two minutes less than the time allowed. It is wise to aim at finishing Section A in one minute less than the time allowed so as to compensate for any possible inaccuracy in the watch used.

Since few horses in driving trials can trot at a speed faster than 20kph (12mph), there is virtually no risk of any competitor finishing Section C in less than the minimum time unless the normal speed for this section is reduced. Even if it is, drivers should trot as fast as their horses can, pressing them to this extent, and take a time check only at the last kilometre marker for reassurance.

There is no minimum time, and there are no kilometre markers in Section E, so any sensible competitor will drive as fast as he can until he is through the last obstacle. After this a time check may possibly tell him that he is able to relax and ease his horses, although this is very unlikely and only possible if the obstacles have taken very little time to negotiate.

The rules demand that a competitor who halts or walks in a trotting section so as to waste time and avoid finishing it too early be penalised for breaks of pace, or at the rate of 1 penalty for every commenced period of 10 seconds spent at the halt. However, he may, without pen-

British National Champion Diane Weston at Sandringham, 1984 *(Leslie Lane)*

alty, circle endlessly at the trot just before the finish of a section if he does need to waste time, and an accurate watch, synchronised with the timekeeper's at the start of the marathon, will show whether this is necessary.

Breaks of Pace

Breaks of pace are deemed to have gained an advantage if they last for more than 5 seconds, and to have taken place if only one horse in a team, pair or tandem breaks. They are penalised, at the rate of 1 penalty for every 5 seconds that they persist, by the referees who accompany teams and horse pairs, and by judges who see them from the ground in the case of other turnouts. Deliberate breaks of pace are liable to incur elimination or even disqualification, and almost certainly will if they occur in walk sections, but referees and judges will normally exercise discretion where horses cannot maintain a trot up or down steep hills or over short stretches of treacherous going.

The different standards applied by different referees with regard to breaks of pace caused constant dispute during the early years of driving trials, but the 5 second rule and the interrogation of referees by the judges at the end of the marathon have greatly reduced inequities in this respect. Breaks of pace are quite unusual now, particularly with experienced competitors who have found that the interruption which they cause to the rhythm of their horses' progress frequently results in loss of speed, quite apart from the risk of penalties. They are probably most likely to occur when drivers are quite legitimately galloping their horses through the final elements of obstacles in Section E and fail to reduce pace in time after crossing the line of the penalty zone.

Halts and Hold-ups

Competitors may halt without penalty in any part of the marathon to repair vehicles or harness but will not be given any time allowance unless they are held up by something beyond their control or involved in an accident for which they are not responsible. In such cases they will be credited with the full time lost and can reasonably expect to receive any allowance which they claim when they have no referee with them and the incident is not witnessed by any judge or steward.

Grooms may, of course, dismount without penalty on such occasions or in any circumstances in the trotting sections of a marathon, provided that they follow the prescribed course on foot and do not shorten it by going the wrong side of turning flags. It costs 20 penalties for a groom to dismount in a walk section.

Errors of Course

The first marathon courses were usually laid out along roads and well-defined tracks which were accurately recorded on maps and, since they were expected to keep to these, competitors were subject to penalties if they deviated from them by more than 10m. This rule, coupled with the one about minimum times which then applied to all sections, created some absurd situations. Competitors who needed to waste time at the end of the obstacle section, after driving as fast as possible until completing the last obstacle to give themselves time in hand in case they got stuck anywhere, were seen by astonished spectators to be finishing by driving a tight serpentine 9m each side of the track at a slow trot.

The rule also caused endless disputes about the exact routes to be taken when these were obscure on the ground and not charted on maps, and led to constant attempts to exercise 'gamesmanship' by competitors who found short cuts and sought to use them on the pretext that the absence of a defined track did not forbid this. Sometimes they took the short cuts and argued vociferously, and often successfully, afterwards. The confusion which resulted from this was resolved by a sensible reversion to the old traditional system, which all horse sports have inherited from racing, that a course must be defined between flags with red ones to be kept on the competitor's right side and white ones on his left. This has caused much extra work for course builders in marking exactly the bounds of courses up to 27km long which must often be illogically tortuous to fit into a restricted area.

A rather jolly, if slightly irresponsible, battle of wits has ensued between course builders and competitors, which the latter have won on the few occasions when the former have failed to block a short cut which has, however, often not been worth taking. The reversion to 'between the flags' has, however, simplified the system admirably in that an error of course, which entails mandatory elimination, can be committed only by missing one of the numbered pairs of flags and the evidence of a referee, judge or steward to this effect is specific and indisputable.

Walk Sections

The walk sections of marathons are valid tests for harness horses which, although most of their work is done at the trot, should be able to walk fast by way of gaining a break and a rest without undue delay on long journeys. They serve also to provide comparative relaxation for ten minutes after the exertions of the trot sections and, together with the ten-minute compulsory halts which follow them, should enable the rates of pulse and respiration to return almost to normal resting levels so that they can be taken into account in veterinary checks for fitness.

For horses, 7kph is a very fast walk, and 6kph is just as fast for very small ponies, so that only a few competitors normally complete these sections without a few penalties. If they are to be fair tests at these speeds, walk sections should be routed over flat ground with firm level going; traffic-free tarmac roads are entirely suitable for them.

Marathon Obstacles

The obstacles in Section E of the marathon are the essence of the course, and thus, basically, of the whole event. Because each second taken to negotiate each obstacle counts one-fifth of a penalty point, they cannot be driven 'clear' and almost always exact a toll of at least 5 penalties each. Course builders always try to provide eight obstacles, so they are

British National Champion Mark Broadbent driving his Welsh Mountain
pony team through the water at Windsor *(Findlay Davidson)*

bound to cost at least 40 penalty points in total and, although the good drivers will often incur no other penalties in the marathon and drive a clear round through the cones in Competition C, this is more than the best of them are likely to score in presentation and dressage.

Although a marathon obstacle may consist of a relatively straightforward crossing of a natural hazard such as water, most of them comprise four or five gates or elements, marked by red flags on their right and white flags on their left, and each lettered in sequence. These must be negotiated in the sequence in which they are lettered. Obstacles may also be composed of unlettered gates or elements to be negotiated in any sequence provided that none is missed. To avoid confusion, obstacles should not include lettered gates as well as unlettered ones and these need not be anticipated by competitors. There is no limit in the rules to the number of gates or elements which an obstacle may contain, but drivers obviously become confused if they have to remember too many in each of seven or eight obstacles.

The compulsory gates in a marathon obstacle are required to be not less than 2.5m wide and, by implication, the whole obstacle should be able to be negotiated correctly without any need to drive through a gap

A particularly difficult marathon obstacle: the 'Puzzle' at the 1982 World Championships at Apeldoorn, Holland

narrower than 2.5m. However, a number of shorter and quicker routes through it will almost certainly incorporate narrower gaps, as well as tighter turning circles and more difficult gradients, leaving a number of different options between short and difficult and long and easy. The skill of the designer lies in ensuring that the long easy routes really do take appreciably longer than the short difficult ones for a good driver to negotiate since, if the difference is only a matter of a few seconds, competitors will not be tempted to take the short routes and risk getting stuck in them.

A penalty zone around each obstacle is marked by a continuous line of sawdust at a distance of 20m from any of the compulsory elements which comprise it. The significance of this is that drivers must keep their whole turnout within the zone until they have completed the obstacle, and incur 20 penalties on each occasion that they fail to do this.

Since 1982 the total length or size of obstacles has been unlimited by the rules and restricted only by their effective configuration and the need for competitors to be timed through them manually to an accuracy of one second.

In 1984 compulsory entrances and exits for obstacles were instituted consisting of wide, flag-guarded gates set in the line of penalty zones. These have made timing easier and more accurate, particularly in cases where the entry gate in reverse can also form the exit, and in many cases the line indicating the remainder of the penalty zone is no longer of much consequence and need not be so clearly indicated or constantly watched by the obstacle judges.

Penalties in Obstacles

The jurisdiction of the obstacle judges supersedes that of referees as soon as a competitor has entered an obstacle and until he leaves it. They must time his passage very accurately through it, since each second that he takes costs one-fifth of a penalty point and scores are recorded to the first decimal point.

They must also ensure that he takes the correct course through it and this entails driving through each gate or element in the right direction in its correct lettered sequence or not missing any in obstacles whose gates or elements are not lettered. As soon as a competitor has driven through a gate it is considered to be completed or 'dead' and may be driven through again in either direction if this helps in an approach to another one. But if a competitor drives or backs right through a gate in the wrong sequence, or from the wrong direction even in the correct sequence, he is deemed to have taken the wrong course and is eliminated and allowed no opportunity to correct his mistake.

He is also eliminated if he has not completed the obstacle within the time limit, which is 5 minutes for all obstacles. In this case only, he will be warned by the obstacle judges when he has only 2 more minutes left so that he may increase his efforts to extricate himself, and be told as soon as the 5 minutes are up that he is eliminated and must leave the obstacle at once and clear the course for other competitors.

For errors of course, or any other mistakes or rule infringements which may entail elimination, a competitor is not told that he is eliminated by obstacle judges or referees, and may continue the course in hope, to be notified of his elimination only at the end of it.

The ruling that a competitor may not rectify an error of course in an obstacle if he appreciates that he has gone wrong and can drive the whole obstacle correctly in a second attempt within the time limit is controversial and has been disputed. The grounds for dispute are that the ruling is based on an interpretation of the particular rule which is inconsistent with the intentions of the general rules applicable to the marathon. These prescribe an exact course to be driven throughout the whole marathon, including the obstacles in Section E, and enjoin penalties, including elimination, for any acts or omissions by which its precise requirements, including the paces decreed, may be reduced or evaded. Subject to these, time is accepted as the ultimate factor in deciding results, and elimination is the penalty for exceeding a time limit.

Since competitors who go wrong on the course by missing turning flags may return and correct their errors without penalties, except loss of time, it is arguable that the same provision should apply to whole obstacles in Section E and that competitors should be allowed to have two or more attempts to drive them correctly within their time limits and lose only time in doing this. There are no suggestions that corrections to errors of course should be allowed to be made piecemeal in respect of the separate elements of an obstacle.

The best drivers are so quick through the obstacles now that a competitor needing to make a second attempt would have virtually no chance of staying 'in the money'; but elimination is a Draconian penalty which is best avoided except in cases where competitors have failed to comply with the requirements of the course or the rules and do not

Deidre Pirie of the United States of America driving her Holstein team in the
World Championships, 1984 *(Findlay Davidson)*

correct their mistakes or cannot do so within the appropriate time
limits.

The elements of marathon obstacles should be unbreakable and
immovable so as to discourage bulldozer tactics and avoid uncertainty
about which side of them horses have passed if they are broken or dislodged. The rules permit up to two obstacles with collapsible elements
in the marathons of trials other than championships and official international ones, and this concession has been used at some English
events, notably those run in conjunction with Royal Windsor Show.

The advantages of collapsible elements are that they can be used to
build a tight, difficult obstacle which may be driven by top-class competitors and novices alike without the risk of the latter being damaged
in them, and they can be easily moved so as to tighten turning circles
and convert obstacles designed for four-horse teams to be equally
effective for pairs and singles. Under British national rules the cost of

knocking down collapsible elements is 10 penalties for each gate involved and this is nearly always enough to deter competitors from hitting them on purpose to save the time which they would have to spend in manoeuvring carefully round them. The concept of knock-down obstacles is, however, basically unsound because if they were to be widely used, designers would inevitably build tight obstacles which would be very difficult to negotiate without penalty. Circumstances would eventually arise in which so many early starters would knock down a gate, despite their best endeavours to avoid this, that later ones might decide to take less trouble about it and at least save time penalties. Thus gamesmanship could quite easily triumph over driving skill.

In an obstacle, it costs 10 penalties to put one groom down, a further 10 to put a second groom down, and a further 10 if the driver has to dismount as well. Curiously, a penalty of 20 points is exacted if the driver puts down his whip. If the carriage overturns a total of 60 penalties is awarded but this covers all the other penalties already mentioned. Horses may not be led out of an obstacle separated from their carriage, on pain of elimination.

If a groom has to get down in an obstacle in a national competition these days it will probably put paid to the chances of that competitor in the event, but to allow horses to struggle for more than a minute or so when the carriage is stuck for want of some help from the ground will cost more penalties in the long run and be unkind and mentally disturbing. The driver must make a fairly instant decision if his vehicle gets stuck, and if a wheel is trapped against a post or tree and the horses cannot back the carriage to free it, a groom must get down to help them.

Provided that nothing is broken and the horses are not unduly upset or out of full control, the immediate action required will almost invariably be to back the carriage about three feet and either pull the pole head well over to free a front wheel or lift the back of it round to free a rear one. A four foot length of rope with a hook or a big eye splice at one end is very useful to attach to the pole head to help with the former operation, and good projecting hand-holds at a suitable height on the back of the carriage will assist the latter one.

Where a team is concerned, a very strong groom can probably do either of these tasks by himself and save the extra 10 penalties for his companion getting down, but two will almost certainly do the job more quickly than one, and may make up most, if not all, of the extra 10 penalties by saving time penalties both through the obstacle and over the whole section. It is futile to have one groom struggling on the

Paul Tointon in an upset at Sandringham. He and his groom were injured but the horses were unscathed *(Leslie Lane)*

ground for two or three minutes while the other watches him from the carriage and finally has to get down to help him, so the decision to dismount one or two should be made in the first instance. Once a groom's foot has touched the ground the 10 penalties are lost and cannot be recovered or added to, so grooms should stay on the ground and lead the horses through the obstacle before remounting.

Reconnaissance of the Course

Competitors now spend far less time making reconnaissances of marathon courses than they did ten years ago — and sensibly, because much of the time which they used to spend grinding tediously along in convoy over perfectly straightforward, clearly-defined tracks, and destroying their surfaces in the process, was wasted. However, time spent in reconnoitring the marathon obstacles is never wasted, and the more so now that their designs are becoming deceptively more sophisticated, with a greater number of alternative routes than in the early days and more reliance on the influence of gradients.

Drivers and their grooms should familiarise themselves completely with the configurations of each obstacle and positively identify the gates and elements and fix them firmly in their minds. This must be done very thoroughly because many distractions will intervene before Section E is actually driven to cause perfunctory perceptions to be forgotten. Drivers should listen to advice from their grooms and friends, and even from other competitors, but must finally make their own firm decisions about the routes which they will take, tell their grooms what they are, and stick to them rigidly once they have completed their reconnaissances.

In making these decisions, drivers should bear in mind that if horses have to be slowed right down to make a tight turn they may take several seconds to get into their stride again and several more, with a risk of jibbing and being unwilling to go forward again at all, if the turn is made on or into a steep slope. Leaders of a team or tandem can be of no help when a tight turn has to be made up a steep slope, and must be kept well out of draught in these circumstances if they are to be prevented from pulling the pole head over and locking the forecarriage against the post round which the turn is being made. When this situation threatens a team must be halted immediately and the leaders must stand quite still with slack traces while the wheelers are moved sideways against the direction of the turn until the relevant front wheel is clear of the post.

HRH The Duke of Edinburgh in an upset at Lowther during his earlier days. The horses were eventually recovered *(Leslie Lane)*

This manoeuvre requires masterly control of a team and the horses will need to respond to the voice as much as to the reins.

Horses in harness can cope with downhill slopes of up to 45 degrees provided that they are not much more than 20m long and so long as four-wheeled carriages concerned have good brakes. They must, however, go straight down them as a traverse across a slope of even 25 degrees can cause most carriages to overturn.

Outside Assistance and Accident Procedure

The rules prohibiting outside assistance are suspended if there is an accident, or the imminent threat of one, regardless of the responsibility for it, so drivers should accept any help offered in these circumstances and tell referees, if they have them, that they propose to do so. The most urgent requirement is to prevent horses running away in panic with an overturned vehicle attached to them and outside helpers should appreciate that it is just as important to restrain the wheelers of a four-in-hand as the leaders. The old recommendation to 'sit on his head' is the best one to adopt to prevent a fallen horse in harness injuring his companions in his struggles to regain his feet, but only experienced people should undo buckles or attempt to remove parts of the harness.

The rules require the same spare harness to be carried at the start of the marathon as for presentation and the judge at the start may award 10 penalties if any of it is missing. First-aid kit is not specified but should certainly be carried for horses as well as humans. It is also very desirable to carry spare shoes. There will usually be a farrier at the second halt, and sometimes at the first one as well, but he cannot be expected to provide shoes to fit all the horses and ponies involved, or even to find one to fit in ten minutes if he does have one. Most horses will probably survive a marathon on a bare sole but the walls of the hoof will become broken and grip will be reduced on hills.

Although fit horses are most unlikely to become exhausted as a result of their exertions during marathons, they can become seriously dehydrated in very hot weather and may suffer from heat exhaustion. Water must be available at both compulsory halts and horses should be allowed to drink up to half a bucketful at each of them. They should be sponged all over with cool water and particularly around their mouths and nostrils at the halts, and a greenhouse syringe with a fine spray may be used to advantage to provide the equivalent of a refreshing shower, even on the move so far as wheelers are concerned.

5

The Obstacle Competition
and Scurry Driving

'*You got it wrong again.*'

The main object of Competition C, the obstacle competition, is to test the fitness, obedience and suppleness of the horses after the marathon, but it is also a trial of skill and competence of their drivers. It is intended to be the counterpart of the show jumping phase of a ridden horse trial and is indeed as nearly as possible related to this for horses which cannot leave the ground.

Both the international and the British national rules permit this competition to be held on its own, and scurry competitions are run under this concession and are bound by driving trials rules with some minor amendments. Under international rules Competition C must always be the last to take place in any trials since one of its main purposes is to

Mavis Clarke with her Lippizzaner pair at Osberton, 1984 *(Sandra M. Caton, Horse & Driving)*

prove that the horses are still fit and willing after the rigours of the marathon. However, a recent amendment to the British national rules permits the organisers of a one- or two-day event to stage it immediately after the dressage and before the marathon so that it may fit more easily into a tight timetable. This also saves competitors the trouble of changing back into their best harness and clothes and cleaning up their horses in a hurry as soon as they have finished the marathon. In this case it has no relevance as a proof of continued fitness but remains a significant extra test of skill and obedience training.

The Course

The essence of the test involved is that competitors are required to drive their horses between pairs of plastic cones, which are set only slightly wider apart than their carriages, over a twisting course at a fairly fast trot. The cones, which in Britain are more usually triangular than

84

conical, are designed so that the rims of the carriage wheels touch them first at ground level before any other part of the carriage can hit them higher up, and are surmounted by balls which fall when this happens.

The cones themselves must be at least 30cm high and those in current use in any country are in fact at least 70cm high so that they can be seen easily by the horses. The rules require that the measurement between each pair of cones shall be not more than 60cm and not less than 30cm greater than the track width of the wheels of the vehicle concerned, measured on the ground. For four-wheeled vehicles the track width of the rear wheels is that which is taken. For pair and single-horsed vehicles the extra width may be reduced to 20cm. The technical delegate decides which of these measurements, in multiples of ten, will apply to each class in the event, and it is constant for each pair of cones in each class. He consults the course builder about this and takes into consideration the difficulty and complexity of the course which the latter has laid out and the standard of skill of the competitors who are to drive it.

Until 1985, one of the biggest bugbears in driving trials was the need to alter the setting of each pair of cones in the obstacle competition to take account of the varying track widths of the vehicles involved. Enforced standardisation of their track widths was contemplated from time to time but rightly dismissed as being an unreasonably expensive demand to make of all competitors and savouring of vandalism where it would have affected the many beautiful old carriages which are driven in Competitions A and C and which lend a touch of unique distinction to these occasions.

The solution to this problem seems to have been found in the devising of a standard width bar, like those which have been in use for some years in scurry competitions, which can be fitted to any vehicle, whether two- or four-wheeled. This enables all vehicles to have the same effective track widths in their respective categories and classes, and research has revealed that the most generally acceptable widths are: 160cm for horse team vehicles, 150cm for all other horse vehicles, and 140cm for all pony vehicles. A number of carts and carriages already fit these measurements but those which do not now have a standard bar fitted for Competition C so that the cones no longer need to be reset except between the relevant classes.

This arrangement greatly reduces the wearisome measuring and remeasuring for the collecting ring stewards, as well as the course builder and his arena party, and removes the risk of a competitor

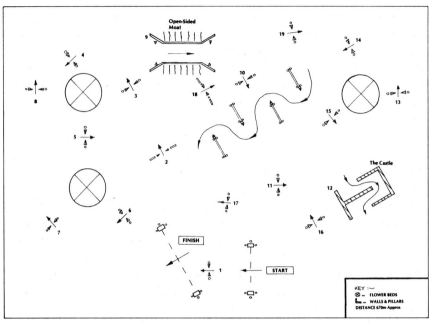

The layout of the 1980 World Championships obstacle course at Windsor

driving the obstacle course with the cones at the wrong setting for his vehicle. This latter mistake occurred very seldom thanks to the conscientious vigilance of the people concerned, but was traumatic when it did and impossible to correct with equal fairness to all the competitors concerned because any who were given a second chance after driving with the cones set wrong had already had a school over the course.

The currently prescribed track widths seem to satisfy the majority of drivers who will undoubtedly have any new vehicles built to comply with them and may gradually convert their existing ones to the required measurements if they want to dispense with the standard bar. Meanwhile, the cones need only be remeasured between classes and if they are displaced, and only the vehicles of competitors who are 'in the money', or likely to be, need be measured, and this after they have completed their rounds.

The length of an obstacle course must be between 500 and 800m, the track being that which a sensible, competent driver would be expected to take from one obstacle to the next around the whole course. Pairs of cones are regarded as single obstacles and the course designer may also lay out or build multiple obstacles in the forms of a water splash, a low wooden or stone bridge, a serpentine consisting of not more than four

86

posts each covered by a cone and its ball, and obstacles involving 'U' turns or 'L' turns normally built of elements of show jumps with three or two pairs of cones incorporated in them. Not more than one water splash and two other multiple obstacles, or three multiple obstacles if there is no water splash, may be included in an obstacle course, and the total number of obstacles, single and multiple, may not exceed twenty. There are exact specifications concerning the measurements of multiple obstacles, the permissible distances between obstacles, and those between the start and finish of the course and the first and last obstacles. Competitors and prospective course builders should study the relevant rule book to learn about these and keep up to date with the fairly frequent amendments which are made to them. There must be no obstacle which requires a driver to rein back to negotiate it since this, in rather incongruous conformity with the rules of show jumping on which the obstacle competition is closely based, is counted as a refusal. There is a more practical reason for this prohibition in that attempts to rein back in a hurry during a competition of this kind are frequently unedifying and rather unkind to the horses.

The ingenuity of the designer of an obstacle driving course is somewhat restricted by the precise rules which circumscribe it, but he can position his cones and his three permissible multiple obstacles so as to form courses which will vary between being virtually impossible to drive at the required speed, and being able to be driven quite easily at a speed of 50m per minute faster than required. For purposes of compiling a timetable, an obstacle competition may be arranged to run at a rate of twenty competitors an hour, or ten competitors an hour including some 'drives-off', provided that the course builder knows the rate at which he is to aim.

Scoring

Each knock-down costs 5 penalty points. Prior to 1984 the cost was 10 penalty points, as in the show jumping phase of the ridden three-day event, but it was reduced from 1984 onwards so as to bring the influence of Competition C into a more balanced relationship with the other two competitions. Only one knock-down is counted for each single obstacle, even if both balls happen to be dislodged, but two or three can be scored for a multiple obstacle which can cost 10 or 15 penalty points if both, or all three, elements are hit.

Stopping, stepping back or circling before an obstacle is counted as

a disobedience or refusal as in show jumping and costs 10 penalties the first time, 20 penalties the second time and elimination for the third time that it happens during a round. One or both grooms dismounting is counted as a disobedience, and penalised as such, so that if horses will not face the water splash, which is normally the only reason for a refusal other than a technical one caused by faulty steering, a wise driver will dismount his grooms immediately to lead the horses through it since the act of a groom dismounting after a second attempt incurs elimination in itself before the obstacle is attempted for the third time. Penalties for refusals, including purely technical ones in which a driver is deemed to have circled before an obstacle if he crosses his track in his approach to it, are cumulative throughout each round with elimination as the invariable penalty for the third one.

Speeds and Timing

The time allowed is calculated to require a speed of 200m per minute for teams and tandems of horses or ponies and 220m per minute for pairs and singles of both. Exceeding the time allowed costs half a penalty point for every second, or commenced period of a second, by which it is exceeded. The time limit is twice the time allowed and exceeding this brings elimination. Taking the wrong course, ie passing through an obstacle out of order, entails elimination as in show jumping.

The starting order for Competition C in a three-phase trial when it is held after the other two is determined by the scores of the previous competitions with the competitor with the most penalty points starting first and the competitor with the fewest starting last.

Clear rounds are fairly common in Competition C of driving trials, as they are in the show jumping phase of ridden horse trials. When separate prizes are offered for the winners of each competition as well as of the whole event, British national rules stipulate that the competitor who has driven the fastest clear round shall be the winner of the obstacle competition, unless a drive-off is held to determine this. When-

Colonel Hywel Davies driving the Household Cavalry team at Lowther, 1983 *(Horse & Driving)*

George Bowman with his Lippizzaner team at Holker Hall, 1984 *(K. G. Ettridge, Horse & Driving)*

ever the timetable of the programme allows for it, a drive-off between the competitors with clear rounds is preferable to determine the placings in Competition C, since this can be unrelated to the results of the main event which will already have been decided. The competitors who have won the main event or been placed in it will have no temptation to drive faster than they need to be within the time allowed to complete the main trial and hold their positions in it, but can show their best speed for the admiration of the spectators in the drive-off. This may legitimately take the form of a time competition over a shortened course in which each knock-down adds a 5 second penalty to the competitor's actual time and the fastest one, on corrected time, wins the competition.

On the unusual occasions when an obstacle competition is run separately from either of the other two competitions and does not form part of a three-phase driving trial, the time competition may, of course, be used for it and will provide a faster more exciting spectacle than the fault one. The starting order for it should be determined by a draw as the last competitor to go has an obvious advantage.

Scurry Driving

The scurry competition brings driving trials into the orbit of the ordinary horse or agricultural show as a simply-staged ring display which provides intermissions between show classes or jumping competitions. Using the same cones as for driving trials, it is governed by the same general rules and is run as a time competition but with refusals discounted so that the whole emphasis is on speed and a very fast driver may win despite two or three knock-downs which each add 5 seconds to his time.

Ten or twelve pairs of cones can be set out in a few minutes in a show ring and, since the competitors' vehicles are fitted with standard scurry bars, they do not need to be reset. The show jumping timing equipment is used, and a class of six or eight competitors, the usual number, can drive against each other and produce a decisive result within twenty minutes of the ring being clear for their performance.

Scurry competitions are open only to pairs of ponies in two classes, over 12hh but not over 14hh and under 12hh respectively, and these, like many good gymkhana ponies, quickly become rather hot and excitable in the ring and unsuitable for driving trials or any other competitive work in harness. Most of their human partners tend also to be specialists, confining their equestrian competitive activities to this one

Tjeerd Velstra, former World Champion, driving his Dutch Warmblood team at Windsor, 1984. These horses were called Gelderlanders until recently but the Dutch have now regularised their nomenclature *(Stuart Newsham, Horse & Driving)*

scene, which can be profitable for those of its twenty-five or so regular participants who are most successful at it, because of the commercial sponsorship which its appeal to the television cameras attracts. The tendency of the four-wheeled scurry carts to be on two wheels for much of their rounds, and not infrequently to turn over, excites many of the people who watch them, offends a few, and leaves their drivers largely unmoved. The ponies concerned certainly earn their keep and seem to enjoy themselves hugely in the process. Scurry driving has been called the stock car racing of horse sport, and the description is a fairly apt one.

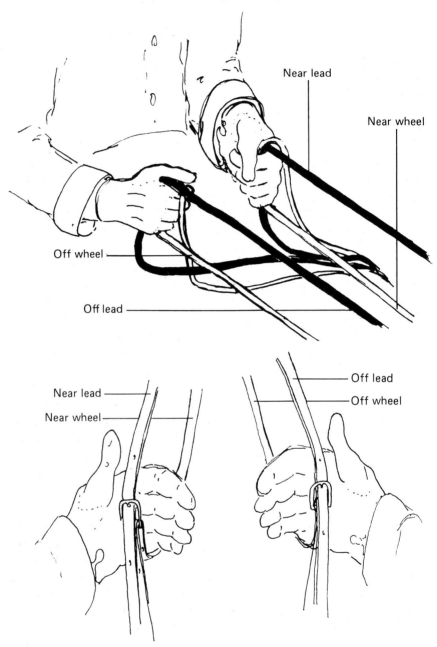

Near lead

Near wheel

Off wheel

Off lead

Near lead

Near wheel

Off lead

Off wheel

The modern two-handed method for a four-in-hand, now much used in Competition C obstacle driving. Buckles (as illustrated) or clamps are often used to prevent the reins slipping and are practical for short periods although they restrict precise rein handling or major adjustments

Steering and Rein Handling

To drive a team or a tandem between a single pair of cones with only 15cm (6in) of clearance on each side of the carriage wheels requires considerable skill and looks much easier to do than it actually is. To steer a pair or a single horse between them is certainly easier by virtue of the lesser length involved and the absence of extra horses out in front and the extra pair of reins. However, many a novice driver will appreciate the difficulty of even driving a dead straight course without a deviation of more than 15cm (6in), with a single horse and no urgency about time, as a measure of the precise and closely co-ordinated rein handling required to drive clear through the twisting offset cones of an obstacle competition course at an average speed of 13kph (8mph).

The leaders of teams, and even more so of tandems who are without the moral support of partners, must display exemplary simple intelligence and a fine spirit of co-operation in responding to signals through the reins which can do little more than point them at the next obstacle. They need to recognise the gap between the markers and trot straight through the middle of it without much further help from their driver, and then to be instantly ready to be turned and pointed at another one.

Meanwhile, an experienced driver of a team or pair will keep his eye on his pole head and concentrate, almost subconsciously, on steering it exactly between the cones. A tandem or single driver will actually be at a slight disadvantage in not having a pole head with which to maintain his aim. He will find it very difficult to watch both his wheels for steering purposes and must generally rely on steering his horse's head exactly between the markers although it will be well above them and not always held quite straight.

Most successful trials drivers have resorted to some form of two-handed driving through the cones. Modified in most cases to allow for a bridge in the Hungarian style so that the reins are not entirely separated, the advantage of this method over the English or Achenbach one for this particular purpose is that it enables turns to be made at less than a right angle more rapidly and rather more precisely, though at the expense of the driver's inability to shorten or lengthen his reins readily through his fingers. By buckling or clamping the reins together, or to a short 'frog' or brezel behind his fingers, a driver can ensure that they will not slip, but he can retain the effective range of the length of either of his arms, increasing it by bending his body forward as required to give and take the reins between the near and offside horses and, to a

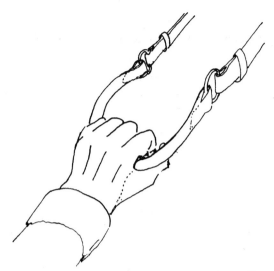

The Hungarian brezel: less used now than in earlier times

more limited extent, to alter the tensions between the lead and wheel horses on either side.

It usually pays to pole up the wheelers of a team or the horses of a pair more tightly than usual to achieve more positive precise steering between the cones. The very slight discomfort which may be caused by pressure on their necks will be of such short duration as to be insignificant. It is also sensible to sit in the middle of the box seat rather than on one side of it.

Walking the Course

Drivers can seldom spend too much time in walking an obstacle course. Since the obstacles largely consist of pairs of identical cones, they are less distinctive than the varied fences of a show jumping course, so that the track is more difficult to recognise and remember. Grooms should also walk it since, although they are forbidden to indicate the course to their drivers, discreet verbal reminders from them will not even be heard by the jury and may be invaluable if given briefly in any moment of mental aberration.

Most of all, drivers should consider and plan their lines of approach to each obstacle and decide where they will make their turns and main changes of direction so as to be squared up on a straight line to them without wasting time by travelling further than necessary or having to pull up or reduce pace unduly. Any pace is allowed in the obstacle competition, so horses can be galloped after the last obstacle and possibly over other parts of the course where the route is straight; and they will need to be galloped in a time competition. However, cantering and galloping does not improve the steering qualities of a horse-drawn carriage so it is wise to moderate the pace through the less straightforwardly sited obstacles and to plan in advance those stretches of the course where it may be increased.

Developments for the Future

The obstacle competition is a good, and even exacting, test of the qualities which it is intended to prove. However, it is unenterprising and unexciting for competitors to drive and deadly dull for spectators to watch. Its close dependence on the format of the show jumping competition, without the vital element of the jumping and the variety of different obstacles which this demands, has reduced it to a very stereotyped procedure with no scope for development or the exercise of ingenuity in its requirements or design. The only real spectator interest which it arouses is the possibility of its effecting a change in the apparent results at the very end of a driving trial, or ending in an accident caused by a competitor going too fast and getting out of control in a drive-off or a scurry competition.

In fact, there were a number of quite amusing competitions, based on the general concept of obstacle driving, run individually by different horse shows in Britain before the advent of driving trials, and plenty of them, offering wide variety, now take place regularly in America under the auspices of the American Driving Society, the Carriage Driving Association of America and various other societies and associations. Of these, a Gamblers' stakes is perennially popular because it necessarily incorporates a wide variety of obstacles and favours boldness on the part of the competitor. Now that the problem of achieving an effective standard track width for all vehicles seems to have been solved, a slight relaxation of the rules could result in the design of more adventurous obstacles and courses which call for changes of pace as well as accurate steering.

In its present form the obstacle competition is a valid test of drivers and their horses, but it comes as an unspectacular anti-climax at the end of a three-day event, particularly for the spectators, and often seems to be hardly worth the extra day devoted to it. Over the years, show jumping has managed to introduce variety and greatly improved spectator appeal into even its standard competitions, without losing its basic aims or sacrificing the essential equity which its rules provide. No doubt its driven counterpart can be induced to develop along the same lines and achieve a similar outcome.

6

Schooling and Fitness Training

'You must pick your feet up . . . like this.'

To be good at driving trials, horses and ponies need to be completely obedient and co-operative, well practised from competitive experience as well as home schooling, and hunting fit. The possession or development of pure physical ability is rather less important to them than to their ridden counterparts, which must jump fences and demonstrate absolute speed, because they are never required to 'leave the ground' — indeed it is usually disastrous if they do — and are not called upon to gallop for more than a few strides.

Obedience and Response to the Voice

Instant and absolute obedience is a prerequisite for all three competitions in driving trials and it must be a willing response to indications and not just a submission to coercion. The only constant contact which a driver has with his horses is through the reins. The whip can and should act as an extension of the driver's arm and hand to correct and to reassure. It can also be used to induce and maintain forward movement, but only very clumsily and imprecisely. It can play no part in regulating or directing movement and is no replacement for the legs and adjusted body weight of a rider in providing aids for the control of his horses.

In harness work the driver's voice is the only replacement for the leg aids and it must invoke instant response. The crucial command is the one to go forward and horses must understand this before any other, but they seem to learn quite an extensive vocabulary of human words and phrases, provided that these are spoken with appropriate inflections by a voice which they recognise. People whose own sensitivity is limited usually underrate the effect of their voices on their horses for the same reason that they often assume that people who cannot speak are also deaf. They frequently cause confusion in their horses' minds by giving vent to their own feelings of anxiety or frustration in a torrent of meaningless exhortations and imprecations.

Obedience to vocal commands and varying rein contact must be learned, in the first instance, by direct association of ideas between these aids and actual compulsion and restraint imposed by the teacher from a firm base on the ground. There is an elementary law of physics involved here to the effect that you cannot lift, move or restrain by direct physical force any animal or thing on which you yourself are sitting. This has been expressed graphically, if facetiously, in the dictum 'You cannot raise yourself from the ground by shortening your braces'.

Since even a very small pony is stronger than a human being and cannot be forcibly manoeuvred against its will, this elementary training should take place as early as possible in a horse's life before it has grown to its full strength and begun to have too many ideas of its own. It is an advantage to have bred your own horse or pony, or have owned it since it was a foal, because nearly all the so-called vices which may develop later on and create problems during advanced training and actual competitions arise largely from misunderstandings, mental confusion, and insensitive handling during the initial stages.

98

Horses should be taught their own names when they are foals and it is obviously undesirable to change them later on. As yearlings they should be taught to move forward on command beside the person who is leading them and to stand still when ordered to do so, if only for thirty seconds at a time. Many other useful practical responses can be taught at this time, such as holding up feet on demand, and they should all be associated with clear distinctive verbal commands.

Young horses can learn a surprisingly large number of simple words and phrases and will remember them all their lives. It is a pity that so much of the vocabulary changes when they are sold to new owners, but educated horsemen generally use much the same one and will advise a new owner about it. Words and phrases can be changed to suit the requirements of new team mates or a new stable, and this is much the same as a child learning a second language.

Preliminary Work on the Lunge

Young horses should be led from both sides and not always on the handler's right as is the usual custom. This will avoid any tendency for them to become one-sided right from the start of their lives and is a precaution which should be observed conscientiously, particularly if they are shown much in hand. This is a consideration which is particularly applicable to horses which are destined for harness work because there will be fewer opportunities for them to be straightened out by a rider's legs later on in their lives than there will be for horses whose work is expected to be under saddle.

Lungeing on a single rein, attached to a cavesson headcollar and not a bit, is the preliminary to long reining in a horse's early training and a useful expedient for providing short exercise periods throughout his life. It is not necessary or desirable to start this work with a harness horse until he is three years old and he should wear protective boots to guard his joints against knocks until he is fit, muscled up and used to the proceedings.

Lunge reins should be at least 9m (30ft) long and made of light webbing or nylon; lampwick serves well provided that it is at least an inch wide. The horse should move in a circle which at first should be not less than 6m (20ft) in diameter. He should circle for an equal time in both directions, changing the rein at intervals of not more than five minutes and for a total session of not more than twenty minutes.

Long Reining

As soon as the horse is going forward freely at the walk and trot and describing a true circle on the single lunge rein, a second rein can be added. The two reins should be attached to each side of the cavesson head collar at this stage and still not to a bit. The horse should wear a riding saddle with the stirrups adjusted to hang just below the flaps and tied to each other under his stomach, and the outside rein should pass through the outside stirrup and lie just above the hocks. This outside rein will start to have a slight effect in bringing the horse's hind legs well under him and preventing him from swinging his quarters out on the circle.

When he is used to the saddle and the outside rein and moving freely on both circles, the inside rein can be led through the inside stirrup and the trainer will be able to restrain forward movement and impose a halt. He should now insist on this at his verbal command and should make the horse stand absolutely still at any point of the circle he may choose for up to one minute, but no longer, before ordering him to go forward again; it is unreasonable to demand complete immobility for more than one minute from a keen young horse.

The next stage is to change the rein by turning the horse inwards and then outwards at the walk and through 180 degrees until he is moving on the opposite circle and, for a harness horse, verbal commands for left and right should accompany this procedure.

The horse can also be taught to rein back with the trainer standing directly behind him and an assistant helping to ensure obedience to the verbal command and the pull of the long reins. This is the stage at which the rein back, like the other requirements, can best be physically imposed. It must be dead straight and for not more than four paces and executed very calmly and patiently so as to avoid the horse suffering any mental confusion in connection with it. It is highly undesirable for the horse ever to move backwards except when asked to do so, or for a greater distance than is asked for, and immediate forward movement must be demanded to correct this tendency if it appears.

The Whip in Lungeing and Long Reining

The trainer needs a long whip with a 1.5m (5ft) stick and a 2.5m (8ft) drop thong; a Hungarian four-in-hand whip is ideal. The whip is essential during early training on the lunge and long reins to enforce instant obedience to the command to go forward. The thong, which will not be heavy enough to cause injury or even pain, must strike the horse's hocks within five seconds of his displaying any reluctance to go forward on command. This situation is virtually the only occasion when the trainer, who may also be the eventual driver of the horse, can seem to his pupil to be in a position to be able to drive him forward physically.

The long whip has many uses, not least that of giving the signals to liberty horses in the circus, but in these circumstances it seems logical to reserve it as a semi-secret weapon to instil a lesson about the apparent omnipotence of the driver which the horse will not be able to fathom or forget and which may avoid many future arguments. If this concept is valid, its efficacy will depend on the trainer keeping the whip well down and behind him and using it circumspectly without showing it to the horse.

An assistant is of great value during the first two or three training sessions, and almost essential if these cannot be conducted in an enclosed manège.

Accepting the Bit

As early as possible in his formal training the horse should become accustomed to wearing harness and having a bit in his mouth. A Liverpool bit with a half moon or Mullen mouthpiece and swivel cheeks is a kind, sensible one for a horse to start his working life with, and there is no real reason why he should ever need another, since he can be ridden with this one as well as driven with it. Fixed cheeks should replace swivel cheeks for pair harness and there may be a change to a Buxton bit for the sake of outward appearance, but the action and effect will not greatly alter. There is no point in introducing a jointed, or broken, snaffle at any stage just to satisfy riding conventions unless the owner has a preference for driving his horse with a Wilson snaffle.

The horse's mouth should not be dry when he has a bit in it and an ordinary curb chain laid along the bar with its ends tied to the rings or cheeks will encourage him to salivate if this is thought necessary. However, it may also tempt him to get his tongue over the bit, an undesirable habit which will be difficult to correct later on, so that this arrangement, or a mouthing bit with special keys, should not be regarded as an essential training aid. The horse should be encouraged to reach for his bit and feel it on the bars of his mouth and he will be helped to do this if it is connected loosely but evenly to the terrets of a harness saddle or by strings crossed over his withers and attached to a stable roller. Tight side reins, particularly if they are fixed lower than the line of the withers, are not a good training aid for a harness horse since they may cause him to bend his neck at the crest and become generally overbent. A correct head carriage with the bend at the poll and the jaw relaxed is crucial to his training and development and this must be achieved by his going forward to accept precise and sympathetic rein contact and not by the imposition of rigid restraint.

Continuation Training

There are three separate procedures which must be undertaken by way of continuation training for a potential driving trials horse or pony: he must be worked in long reins on the bit; he must be ridden; and he must be driven to a vehicle. The horse must expect to be subjected to all three of these experiences by way of more advanced schooling for the rest of his competitive life so it seems logical that he should be introduced to them without undue delay. There is, however, a school of thought which contends that he is likely to be confused by such varied attentions being practised upon him simultaneously, and that he should spend one year learning to pull a cart and a second year learning to carry and respond to a rider. No one doubts, in any case, that long reining from the ground must continue in conjunction with either of the other forms of schooling. On balance it seems that the extra interest and variety in the horse's life engendered by his performing the three different activities each week outweighs in value any advantages there may be in concentrating on one form of schooling at a time.

Long Reining on the Bit

Although a sensible amateur with little or no previous experience will not do much harm in trying to teach himself to lunge or long rein a horse with the reins attached to a head collar, driving a horse on the bit from the ground is a craft which must be learned by apprenticeship. It takes at least ten hours of concentrated practice on an old horse under supervision to perfect the technique, and this presupposes that the operator is quick on his feet and has sympathetic hands and good reactions. More harm than good will result from the inept efforts of an aspiring trainer to teach himself and his young horse from a book or even a film.

The Danish method, which has been demonstrated in England by

Mr E. Schmit Jensen and Miss Sylvia Stanier as well as Mrs Cynthia Haydon with her Hackneys, is probably the best for harness horses. In it, the long reins pass through the terrets of an ordinary driving saddle or pad and then straight to the trainer's hands; the outside rein does not pass round the horse's haunches or hocks. This method provides for precise control with light contact and, since the effective line of the reins is the same as that which will apply when the horse is driven to a vehicle, an appropriate head carriage for harness work will be encouraged.

The English method, with the reins passing through the stirrups or through Ds on a roller at an equivalent height, has the advantage of encouraging active hock action and preventing the horse swinging his quarters out. It should be used in the very early stages without connection to a bit, as previously described, and may be reverted to temporarily, with or without a bit involved, to correct specific faults. However, it tends to create unduly low head carriage and over-bending and, because the reins encounter more friction, contact with the horse's mouth is less light and precise.

Long reining on the bit should normally start about three weeks after first training has begun, provided that there has been no interruption to the programme and the horse has become accustomed to his bit. It is sensible for a harness horse to wear a blinkered bridle from now onwards so that he will get used to it and because it will help him to ignore distractions and concentrate on his work. He should wear his ordinary driving bit, with the reins in the 'smooth cheek' position, and a loosely fitted curb chain, which will not operate or irritate him in any way with the reins so fixed, should be attached after the first few training sessions.

Long reins in fairly expert hands can be used to school horses to a very high level of training, and they can be used to eradicate most faults, particularly those stemming from disobedience. They can be used to correct a faulty head carriage and can be very helpful in improving a horse which is 'one sided' and irregular in action as a consequence. The collected trot can be taught most effectively in long reins because the trainer is well situated to be able to set up the necessary impulsion and control it precisely from his firm position on the ground. A good extended trot can also be developed in long reins but this requires an agile operator who can react and move very quickly and it is more difficult to achieve and less certain to be successful.

A horse which moves sluggishly or clumsily at the trot may have his action improved by being long reined or even lunged over cavalletti.

They should be set at their lowest height, about 15cm (6in) above the ground, and placed at an equal distance from one another — from 1m (3ft 6in) for small ponies to 1.5m (4ft 6in) for big horses. Not more than five cavalletti should be used in one sequence and they must either follow the curve of the circle or be positioned at right angles to the wall or rails of a manège, in which case the trainer must keep pace with the

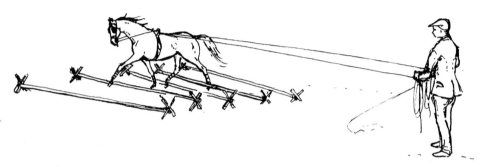

Long reining a driving horse over cavaletti; this can improve the horse's action

horse. Distances between them may be reduced by 30cm (1ft) to induce elevation in collected trot or increased by 30cm (1ft) to encourage the horse to extend his stride. This is an advanced exercise which should be attempted only by an experienced trainer with a calm, well disposed horse.

In short, almost anything which can be taught to a horse by a rider on its back can be taught to it by a driver with long reins on the ground, and often more easily and effectively, particularly when any conflict of wills is involved. Driving trials competitors who hope to be successful will want to put their horses back into long reins for short reschooling sessions at regular intervals throughout their careers. These will be particularly significant and more frequent if competent riders are not available and, in the case of small ponies, this is likely to be usual rather than exceptional.

Riding the Harness Horse

The process of backing horses and accustoming them to work under saddle is exactly the same for harness horses as for riding ones. It is fully explained in many books but beyond the scope of this one. Further training under saddle should be along conventional school riding lines except that work on two tracks and at the canter is unnecessary and probably undesirable, and a vocal command should always immediately precede any leg aids or changes of pace. Apart from the actual schooling involved, harness horses benefit from the variety brought into their lives by being ridden out for exercise at least once a week. There is no harm in their galloping and jumping fences and they will enjoy hunting in the winter when the driving season is over.

The Horse in Draught

The process of breaking a horse to harness and accustoming it to pull a cart is explained fully and clearly in a number of books on this subject, of which the most recent ones are those by Mrs Sallie Walrond. Common sense and horse sense should dominate these proceedings, which can reasonably begin as soon as the horse is working satisfactorily in long reins and has accepted the control imposed by the reins attached to the bit. The driver needs an active assistant throughout all stages of this training and will be well advised not to drive his young horse unaccompanied until he is sure that it is thoroughly used to the vehicle and harness and has overcome any fear of traffic and alarming sights and sounds which it is likely to encounter. This period will be at least twelve weeks from the start of road work in harness and may extend to twenty weeks or more in the case of an unusually nervous horse. It is often very difficult to get a competent assistant, particularly when he or she will be required almost every day, but it is folly to try to manage without one. Situations will inevitably arise which can only be coped with effectively by a second person going quickly to the horse's head to calm and restrain him and failure to provide for this may result in him getting out of control and running away in blind panic dragging an upturned cart behind him. Even if the horse survives uninjured, the risk of injury to other people is considerable and the consequent trauma will remain in his mind for the rest of his life and may seriously affect his temperament.

Horses should wear a well-fitted full neck collar for their first efforts in draught since this spreads the load more evenly and minimises the risk of any temporary discomfort to tender flesh. However, if the neck collar does not fit really well, a breast collar is better. It is just worth while running two poles through the tugs on the driving saddle to accustom the horse to shafts. These, and light ropes attached to the hame draught eyes in lieu of traces, should be held behind the horse in such a way that they can be slipped out and removed if he becomes frightened. By pulling back on the traces the trainer can invite the effort required to pull a light cart. A third assistant will be useful at this stage because there must be one at the horse's head with a leading rein attached to the headstall, as well as the driver/trainer at the end of the reins.

A light vehicle should replace the poles and ropes as soon as the latter are accepted, probably after only two or three sessions, and it is worth having this pushed with the horse in position but not attached to it until

A horse being accustomed to shafts and traces

he has overcome his initial suspicion of it. With most horses this will only be a matter of minutes. Personally, I like the horse to be introduced to the cart, this first time only, without blinkers so that none of this potentially alarming arrangement is concealed from him. It is a fallacy to suppose that blinkers are intended to prevent him from seeing the wheels of his own cart turning behind him, and a horse so stupid as to be unable to realise that he is pulling it himself after doing this for a very short time, would be useless for driving trials and a menace on the roads.

A horse should only be asked to pull a light weight on firm level ground for the first few weeks of his training in draught. Any demand for undue effort at this stage may cause discomfort or even hidden injury to his shoulders and induce the habit of jibbing which may recur most inconveniently at intervals throughout the rest of his life. The cart and passengers should not weigh much more than the horse or pony at any time and steep hills and soft going should be avoided for at least eight weeks after his introduction to pulling it.

An old fashioned but sensibly effective way of teaching a horse to pull a cart is to put him straight into pair harness with a schoolmaster or 'brake horse'. The latter must be absolutely steady and reliable, and stronger than his pupil, and the cart, or brake, must also be very strongly built but not too heavy since for the first few outings the pupil's efforts may well hamper rather than assist those of the schoolmaster. This system was the one normally used by jobmasters and transport contractors for breaking young horses to harness a hundred years ago and, provided the equipment and the essential 'schoolmaster' are available, it has the dual advantage of providing a reassuring initiation into road and traffic conditions as well as work in draught. It is particularly applicable to horses which are intended to form members of a pair or team, and they can be introduced to single harness without much trouble at any time after their apprenticeship in pair harness has been well started.

Introduction to Trials

Advanced schooling for driving trials can best be done at small novice events, or in conditions which simulate them. It is a mistake to practise actual dressage tests more than about once a week because, unless they are varied constantly, a horse will learn a specific test and begin to anticipate its movements. This is undesirable when he is concentrating on the test which is required, and disastrous when he is remembering a different one. The individual movements should be practised out of their original context and order of execution, and not only in a regular arena.

It is well worth acquiring a few obstacle driving cones since horses quickly learn to recognise them and go straight through the middle of them when they are set out in pairs, and they can also be used most effectively to fill in the critical elements of simulated marathon obstacles. Traffic cones, though rather too low and inconspicuous, are a good substitute.

Water Obstacles

There are very few driving trials in which horses do not have to go through water and it is important to remember that the deeply-rooted instinct which prevents their getting themselves and their riders

HRH The Duke of Edinburgh driving the Queen's Oldenburg cross Cleveland Bay mares through the water in Windsor Park. Prince Philip is very good at schooling his horses to be bold through water *(Leslie Lane)*

Opposite British National Champion Sarah Garnett with her attractive tandem in the National Championships, 1983. It is important to get horses accustomed to water, and these actually love it in the course of a hot marathon *(Horse & Driving)*

drowned in bogs on Dartmoor is the same one which inhibits them from stepping boldly into muddy ponds which form elements of competition courses. Their reluctance to do this must be overcome with sympathy and patience.

To avoid the extra complications of the carriage, they should be ridden following a lead from an experienced horse and, to begin with, only into streams or clear pools with a firm visible bottom. An intelligent horse will soon learn to recognise a water obstacle which is part of a marathon course and will trust his driver to commit him to it even if he cannot see its bottom. No water obstacle in driving trials is supposed to be more than 40cm (16in) deep but many inevitably have a greater depth than this, which is only that of an averaged-sized puddle. Even small ponies can safely negotiate water which is 60cm (2ft) deep or a little more, provided that the bottom is firm and clear of large stones or boulders, and the more varied their experience of it can be at home the more confident they will be when meeting it at trials.

It is, however, unwise to drive horses in harness into water more than 90cm (3ft) deep because some of them will instinctively plunge or even try to swim and may get their legs caught up in their harness in the process. The wheelers of a team, in particular, will almost certainly get their forelegs over the swingle trees or pole straps if they strike out in this way. When this happens they will lose their footing and become cast in the water, sometimes with their heads under it with consequent risk of drowning. They will always remember such an alarming experience and may well panic if asked to face water again.

Marathon water obstacles often require competitors to drive along streams and around flags in them rather than straight across them. Since the natural reaction of horses is to get across streams as quickly as possible, even to the extent of trying to jump them, it is necessary to curb this tendency in training and persuade them to walk calmly into water and be willing to turn and circle in it. This lesson is easier to teach in hot weather and when horses are thirsty and can be allowed to stop and drink.

Professional Trainers

Perhaps the most practical advice which may be offered to a keen trials driver is that he should consider having the preliminary training and schooling of his young horses done by a good professional. There are still a few of these valuable people in Great Britain and their charges, which still seem to be very moderate by present-day standards, are usually well justified by the results which they achieve. They bring to their task the great advantages of having the right facilities and equipment and a routine of work which enables them to pursue a regular training programme without interruptions.

Since horses' temperaments are unpredictable, trainers cannot be expected to guarantee specific results within a definite time, but a horse which has been with a professional trainer for six weeks can usually be returned to its owner in a state in which it can be driven quite safely on public roads and in company with other horses by a competent amateur. After twelve weeks, a good professional should have a horse ready for its first novice driving trial and may well be willing to demonstrate this by competing with it himself. Most conscientious trainers will be willing to do a deal with an owner whereby they undertake to produce his horse at an agreed standard of schooling, irrespective of the time this may take, for a fee for the job plus normal livery charges.

In a 'do-it-yourself' age, owners whose pride may inhibit them from getting someone else to train their horses for them may reasonably reflect that their primary endeavour is to determine which rein to pull, and when and how strongly and for how long to pull it, so as to steer the right courses at the correct speeds in driving trials. The problem of ensuring that horses respond readily to these pulls on their reins may be regarded as requiring a slightly different skill and a busy person may not have time to perfect his knowledge of both.

Getting the Horse Fit

Hunting fit is a state of physical well-being recognised by hunting people which enables a horse to carry a rider for five hours at varying paces across country over a total distance of about thirty miles. The horse will endure periods of extreme exertion in jumping fences and galloping through soft going, and the essence of his state of fitness must be that he will not become so tired as to risk suffering strains, sprains or any exhaustion and will be fit and fresh to do the same thing again three or four days later. This routine will last from October to April without any prolonged periods of rest and, although he will usually finish the season leaner than when he started it, he must not lose condition or become obviously thin.

The process of getting a horse into this state of fitness, and keeping him in it, is not quite the same as that which prepares him for a series of efforts which are to take place during a limited period, since this envisages building him up to a peak and letting him down after it. A hunter must face more tests of endurance than a driving trials horse, and more severe ones, but the latter must pull out sound and fresh for the obstacle driving the day after his marathon and cannot have three days to recover from his exertions, so that the standard of fitness required is about the same for both.

It takes at least eight weeks for a horse to get fit enough for even a

Alwyn Holder with his Welsh Cobs at Wylye, 1983. Alwyn is a fine natural horseman who is consistently successful in marathon, and gets his horses wonderfully fit *(K. G. Ettridge, Horse & Driving)*

three-section marathon, assuming that he is quite unfit to start with and is expected to maintain the required speeds in the competition. It is better not to be too rigid or dogmatic in recommending a training programme to cover these eight weeks because it must be influenced by many factors: the experience and need for further education of the horse, and of the driver; the training facilities and the terrain where the work is to take place; the time that the trainer has available and the time of day that suits him best; the weather in general and its variations from day to day. Some guidelines should, however, be laid down, even if some of them may amount to counsels of perfection.

Horses should be worked or exercised every day and two short spells, morning and afternoon, are better than one long one. Two three-quarter-hour periods or one one-hour period a day will suffice for the first week. These should consist mainly of walking, with only three or four spells of working trot lasting not more than three minutes each, and normally in conjunction with dressage training. The horse will cover a total distance of not more than three miles during each of these first week periods, of which at least half should be away from the manège or schooling field.

The daily exercise should be increased to two one-hour periods or one one-and-a-half-hour period in the second week, to two one-and-a-half-hour periods or one two-hour period in the third week, and to two two-hour periods or one three-hour period in the fifth week. From the sixth week onwards the horse will benefit by being at daily work for two two-and-a-half-hour periods or one four-hour period as often as possible. Many owners may be unable to devote this amount of time to the job on a regular basis, so that a practical routine will envisage the horse being at work or exercise for a total of between fifteen and thirty hours each week with no period lasting more than five hours. The ratio of trotting to walking should be increased progressively each week so that by the start of the seventh week as much time should be spent at the trot as at the walk and the horse will be covering twenty miles or more during a good day's work.

Rest Days, Ratios and Limitations

Horses appreciate a regular routine and do not benefit from a day of rest spent confined to their stable. Owners who want this for their own sakes may consider turning their horses out in a well-fenced paddock for three or four hours on the day in question. The horses will not exercise themselves in this situation and there is a risk of their being kicked by any companions which are out with them, but the pleasant holiday atmosphere may just make this worth taking. Two consecutive days with no work or exercise will set the training back significantly and three or more may disrupt it quite seriously from a mental as well as a physical point of view.

The ratio of ridden work to driven work for a horse whose basic schooling is completed may reasonably be from a quarter to a half, and even a well-schooled horse will benefit from a fortnightly session in the long reins, the more so if he cannot be ridden at least once a week.

Horses in harness should not be asked to face steep hills until they are becoming fairly fit, which will be in about the fifth week of preparation. By the same token, they should not be trotted fast on hard roads until their muscles begin to harden at about the same period. They will, however, benefit from a weekly gallop, quite fast for about six furlongs on good going, with a fairly light rider from the sixth week onwards.

In general it is best to do the disciplined work, such as dressage schooling, at the beginning of an exercise period and allow the more relaxed activities to follow it. The idea of taking the edge off a horse's keenness, or even allowing him to settle thoroughly, before attempting any precision work is a bad one because he must learn to be obedient even when he is fresh and rather excited; not just when he is slightly tired. He will undoubtedly be more excited in the atmosphere of an event than at home and will not have time to dispel his surplus energy between his presentation and his dressage test.

It is important to keep the weight of the cart and its occupants to a minimum during training and even ordinary exercising, particularly for small ponies. As explained in Chapter 4, the effort required increases very sharply when horses have to pull a weight equal to or approaching their own up hills or through deep going, and it is not sensible to overload them in training. The ratio is more favourable with pairs and even more so with teams, but a team marathon vehicle weighing 600kg (12cwt) may be unduly heavy for a pair for exercise.

Byways and Green Lanes

It is usually pleasanter to drive along traffic-free rides and tracks than tarmac roads, and trotting at full speed on hard unyielding surfaces for any length of time is not good for horses' feet and legs, even if they are not carrying a weight on their backs. The problem of finding green lanes of this description and being allowed to use them may seem to be considerable, but there are in fact between thirty and forty thousand miles of byways in Britain whose surfaces are unmetalled and which are open to horse-drawn, but not motor, vehicles. These are in addition to the many more bridleways, which are not negotiable by any vehicles, and the county bridleways officers of the British Horse Society, who are unpaid volunteers, will be helpful about showing them to responsible drivers who want to make use of them.

Fitness Indicators

There are several recognisable indications of a horse's state of fitness. He should be well covered but with his muscles discernible and not concealed by fat. There should be a noticeable line below his rib-cage indicating a flat rather than an unduly rounded stomach. All horses sweat, and some more than others, but the sweat of an unfit horse forms a white lather while that of a fit one is clear and makes him seem only damp.

If a weighbridge is accessible, it is interesting to note how a horse's weight varies in accordance with his state of fitness. A fat horse will probably lose weight during the first two or three weeks after he starts work but will usually start to regain it, though more steadily, after this until he reaches a fit weight after seven or eight weeks which may well be greater than his unfit one.

More precise indications are provided by variations in pulse and respiration rates and, to a very limited extent, by alterations in temperature. A resting horse should have a pulse rate of between 34 and 40 beats a minute and a respiration rate about one-third of this frequency. It is not possible to be more exact than this, because the pulse rate, though not the respiration rate, can increase temporarily by up to 10 beats a minute in response to some mental stimulus undetected by human observers. During strenuous exertion, as in a race, the pulse rate may increase to 120 beats a minute or even a little more, and the respiration rate may be about 60 beats a minute or a little more than half the pulse rate. A constantly significant factor is that the respiration rate should never begin to approach that of the pulse; if it does, all work should be stopped and veterinary advice ought to be sought.

A horse's standard of fitness may be quite accurately determined by noting the time which is taken after strong exercise for his pulse and respiration to return to their normal resting rates. In the case of a very unfit horse, this may take thirty or forty minutes, but as fitness improves the period will reduce until it is only about ten minutes. The rate to which the pulse will increase also reduces for the same length and intensity of work as the horse gets fitter. Thus an unfit horse may have a pulse rate of 110 beats to the minute and a respiration rate of 55 after trotting fast for 1km and will not regain his normal resting rate for thirty-five minutes but, after 5 weeks of regular exercise, his rates may be only 75 and 24 after the same 1km at the same speed and will probably drop to 40 and 15 after a ten-minute rest. These criteria can be used to monitor the distances and speeds to which horses may reasonably be subjected in training, and this is the concept of interval training. An exertion which increases the pulse to 85 and the respiration to 35 would not be unreasonable, and the vet at a marathon halt would have

115

no reason to be concerned if he found a rate of 75 and 30 towards the end of the prescribed ten minutes.

The pulse can most easily be felt just inside the horse's lower jaw and the respirations can be seen by watching his nostrils or flanks. Timing of either should be for at least thirty seconds to ensure reasonable accuracy. An expensive device called a Hippocard, involving electrodes attached to a horse's head and breast bone, can be used to read his pulse rate instantly on a dial while he is moving, but this is not an essential piece of equipment.

A horse's temperature may rise one or two degrees above the normal of 37.8°C (100°F) during exertion in hot weather, but there need be no cause for alarm unless it exceeds 38.9°C (102°F).

Horses which sweat freely and compete in driving marathons in very hot weather may become dehydrated with serious consequences. Absence of saliva and a flaccid condition of the skin are telltale symptoms of this. A reasonable drink and a good sponging at each halt will normally cope with this threat but, in extreme conditions, it may be desirable to add some proprietary electrolyte to the water.

If a horse seems to be persistently out of condition and making no progress in his fitness training it may well be wise to arrange for his blood to be analysed. This is essentially a matter for a veterinary surgeon.

Feeding for Fitness

Feeding horses is a very individual skill which is better learned by apprenticeship and from experience than out of books or any of the plethora of commercially-inspired pamphlets which circulate so widely. Even the few ponies which are not intended to take driving trials very seriously should not compete off grass, and all concerned need to be stabled and fed on hard feed.

Very few horses or ponies will eat more of even the best hay than is good for them, so they can safely be kept 'hayed up'. The old job-masters' rule of 1lb of oats for every mile of work, calculated on an average daily basis from a forecast of the next week's work to come, is as good a rule of thumb as any. The rate must be halved for ponies, and the rule can be adjusted to apply to nuts and other patent feeds.

A salt lick is essential but most other supplements and additives probably appeal more to horses' owners than to the animals themselves. 'Little and often' is the other well-tried rule for feeding horses,

116

and concentrates should be fed in anticipation of work to be done not as a replenishment for energy already expended.

Clipping

It always seems a pity to clip into a summer coat and this can sometimes be avoided if horses and ponies are kept well rugged up in March and April and regularly strapped with a rubber currycomb to shift the loose hairs of the old winter coat. A winter coat clipped out at any time before Christmas grows again within three weeks, so it can more happily be sacrificed to the comfort of any of the remarkable native ponies who seem to grow one in early September. Apart from the comfort and the cosmetic angle, a long woolly coat is most unhelpful in keeping a horse or pony in good fit condition for a marathon, so it must come off if it cannot be kept at bay.

Shoeing

A good conscientious blacksmith is the most valuable ally that any competitive driver, or rider, can have. They are rarer and far busier than veterinary surgeons or nagsmen. The job is a lifelong expert study and an owner who manages to get himself onto the books of a good farrier should take advice from him and not try to give it to him. Some elementary recommendations, however, may be incontestable.

Weight on a horse's feet will slow him and tire him much more than weight which he may carry anywhere else on his body, so heavy shoes are a great mistake and any theories about specially weighted ones improving a horse's action are not relevant to driving trials.

Marathon courses usually exclude slippery tarmac roads but these may inevitably be encountered at home, so most owners like to have some extra grip incorporated on their hind shoes. Mordax studs have stood the test of time and always satisfied their users, but they do the job almost too well and dig into tarmac so abruptly that jar is transmitted to horses' legs. This is not of much consequence where the hind shoes are concerned, and it is nearly always the hind feet which slip up, but horses which are shod with studs in front quite quickly seem to lose their action and may also suffer from sore shins and other disabilities caused by the inevitable concussion.

An alternative to studs is borium, which provides a good non-slip surface on the bottom of horse shoes and grips the ground almost as well, without quite the same effect of sudden jarring. It can be used on the front shoes as well as the hind ones and, though expensive to apply, makes them last longer so may almost pay for itself. Some patent ready-made shoes are now sold which incorporate this useful substance.

Horses' shoes, and in particular the nails which secure them, bed down onto a horse's feet very satisfactorily after they have been in use for twenty or thirty miles of road work. For this reason it is better not to have horses newly shod immediately before a driving trial; there will be far less risk of losing a shoe at a critical moment if it has already been in place for a week or so.

7

Ways and Means

'We made the gig ourselves.'

The cynic who compared ocean racing to standing under a cold shower tearing up £5 notes might reckon that people who compete with four-horse teams in driving trials have chosen the most expensive form of transport ever known to man. At £100 or more a mile for the actual distance covered at events, he might well be right, but people with faint hearts or thin purses should probably not contemplate the calculations involved. Although most people will not need or want to know their costs on any sort of a mileage basis, those who may be considering taking up driving trials will certainly need to have some idea of the capital outlay and the annual running costs which they may expect to face, and those who are already facing them may want some basis for comparison, if only by way of reassurance.

Prices of Driving Horses and Ponies

Horses and ponies are relatively cheap to buy in Great Britain because we are over-producing them to an irresponsible extent and a buyer who wants one for driving trials may be bidding only against the meat merchants. The internationally recognised height division between horses and ponies is 148cm or 14.2hh and £800 for a horse or £500 for a pony can easily secure an animal which will go to the top in driving trials. Indeed, several well-known current performers were bought originally at prices slightly below these and have increased their value very considerably through their own abilities and the skill of their drivers. As in all horse dealing, the sky is the limit, but there is no need to think of paying more than £2,000 for a single horse or £1,500 for a single pony except in the case of trials winners or actual or likely show ring winners, or those with breeding potential.

There is a premium on matched pairs which is accounted for by the extra trouble their owners have taken to breed them carefully to look

Peter Munt in the sandpit of the Windsor marathon. These Hungarian Magyarfelver horses were jointly owned by Peter and Stefan van Kaltenborn. He now has a new Swedish team *(Leslie Lane)*

Former Hungarian World Champion György Bárdos at Windsor in 1980 with his Hungarian Lipizzaner team *(Stuart Newsham, Horse & Driving)*

alike or to search the country for a duplicate to the original. This latter undertaking is much more difficult and time consuming than it may seem since the most important factor is that the horses should match in action, and this cannot be determined by direct comparison of measurements or even photographs. It is seldom worth anybody's while to invite descriptions from vendors and make special journeys to see whether the horses on offer match the one at home. A pair is usually only acquired in this way by a person with a good eye for a horse who sees a great many of them in the course of his daily life and has some luck.

A well-matched pair of ponies is worth upwards of £2,000 and a good horse pair is likely to cost £3,500 or more. In tandem horses need not match so well as in pair harness, although their action should still be comparable, so prices relevant to single horses and ponies are applicable to them unless they are already going well together — in which case the leader, in particular, may be worth at least an extra £500. It is also worth paying rather more for the wheeler than his value as a single horse so as to keep a successful combination together.

Since the rules for pairs and tandems allow one reserve horse to be entered and substituted at the start of any competition , this should also be considered by a dedicated trials driver who wants to cover all eventualities in reckoning his costs. In practice, however, the third horse is seldom better than either of the other two in any of the three competitions and is likely to be needed only if one goes lame. When this is not the case he poses a considerable extra problem as regards work and exercise and will usually be embarrassingly superfluous. Most trials drivers accordingly rely on only two horses or ponies for pairs or tandems and revert to entering a single turnout if one animal happens to go lame.

The problem of matching a four-in-hand is commensurately greater than that of matching a pair and, although slightly more difference in build and height is acceptable between wheelers and leaders than between the off-side and the near-side horses, the difficulty of achieving uniformity is understandably reflected in the cost.

A team of four well-matched horses will cost at least £7,500, even if they are just going quietly together and have no performance record, and this price will rise to £10,000 or more if they have any competitive form.

A pony team should cost considerably less than this, although their owners will be loath to admit it, because we have almost a glut of native ponies in England, particularly of Welsh sections A, B and C, and they are therefore easier to match. Four nicely-matched ponies going well together in harness may be bought for £5,000 and they will be worth another £1,500 or £2,000 with a few reasonably successful trials behind them.

The rules applicable to teams of four horses or ponies permit six to be entered for an event and five to be brought to it, so that the fifth or reserve one may be substituted at the start of any of the three competitions. This substitution is allowed without any veterinary recommendation and even if the other four are all sound. This provision is much more significant for teams than it is for pairs and tandems, and a serious competitor may often want to make use of it only because he has a lame horse and cannot compete with only three.

Since all the horses must be exercised equally if they are to be ready for use, it is more practical to work six as a team and a pair than five, and only slightly more expensive to keep the extra two than the extra one. Thus a full establishment will consist of six horses or ponies, but the extra two, as adjuncts to the basic four, will probably not be so well matched and not increase the capital cost by more than £2,000–£3,000. The extra two ponies should not cost more than £500–£750 each.

Thus the essential equine partners for a driving trials competitor will cost him from £500 for a single pony to £20,000 for the six horses needed to establish a four-horse team of championship standard.

Suitable Breeds

Which breeds of horses and ponies are most suitable for driving trials is a perennially fascinating question which, rather happily, remains largely unanswered. Of the sixteen breeds of light horses and ponies in Britain, all have taken part in trials, and twelve of them with some measure of success.

Welsh cobs and ponies have dominated the English scene by weight of numbers as well as wins scored, and Hackney horses and ponies have the highest average of successes in relation to entries, apart from HM The Queen's home-bred Cleveland Bay x Oldenburg horses, which can really be regarded as English because their Oldenburg parentage contains so much thoroughbred and Cleveland Bay blood.

Of the seventy-odd continental breeds west of Russia, nearly half have taken part in driving trials, at least in their own countries, and nearly twenty have had international success.

Hungarian Magyarfelver horses have probably won more competitions than any others. These are a composite type of horse rather than a pure breed and are based on the blood of the Anglo-French horse Nonuis, whose outcrossings with several different breeds at the beginning of the nineteenth century established the prolific line which bears his name and is synonymous with the Hungarian horse. The thoroughbred Furioso and the Norfolk roadster North Star were used on Nonuis mares extensively rather later in the 1800s and later still their progeny were crossed with more English thoroughbreds to create quality horses with substance, calm temperaments and great presence which now breed true to type and have most of the characteristics of middleweight hunters.

Hungarian Lipizzaners, rather bigger than the Austrian type and owing this to admixtures of Kladruber and Orlov trotter blood, have scored the best averages of any breed. This is because they have been driven by three World Champions, Sandor Fulop, Imre Abonyi and György Bárdos, as well as other top-class Hungarian drivers, and latterly by England's George Bowman, but they do have all the right attributes, chief of which is a courageous but calm and intelligent temperament.

Holstein, Hanoverian and Oldenburg horses from Germany, and Dutch and Swedish warmbloods now all have the right proportion of thoroughbred blood to add the necessary quality and high courage to their original substance and sangfroid, and have proved this in national and international trials.

Polish Wielkopolska horses, another comparatively new brand name denoting a careful compound of several different breeds, have true quality and notable powers of endurance inherited from their East Prussian Trakhener forebears.

English drivers who have bought teams of horses in Hungary, Holland and Sweden, and Americans who have imported them from Germany, have done their shopping in an expensive market but generally been well satisfied with the results. State studs with consistently established breeding policies offer horses of uniform type and conformation, usually from stock of proven performance. The facility of being able to see and try four or more nearly identical horses all together in one place, and to buy them from one vendor, may very well be worth the fairly high cost of this arrangement, which is likely to amount to about £3,000 for each horse.

Vehicles

A cart for a single pony suitable for driving trials will cost between £500 and £1,000. The rules stipulate that it must have a track width not less than 115cm and for the obstacle competition (Competition C) the track width must be standard at 140cm. The measurement for Competition C may be achieved by the fitting of a standard bar to increase the effective track width, so that there may be a small advantage in having as narrow a cart as possible for the marathon.

The same measurements are stipulated for four-wheeled vehicles for pony pairs and teams, with the distance between the rear wheels being the relevant one, and for two-wheeled vehicles for pony tandems. The track widths for all vehicles for horses are 125cm for the marathon (Competition B), and 160cm for teams and 150cm for pairs, tandems and singles for Competition C. Telescopic axles are permitted but are now only an expensive alternative to a standard bar.

Minimum weights are stipulated for vehicles in all classes for the marathon only and these can include all equipment carried but not the people. They are: horse teams 600kg, pony teams 300kg, horse pairs 350kg for international trials but 300kg for national ones, pony pairs 225kg for international trials and 200kg for national ones, horse tandems 170kg and pony tandems 110kg (no separate international weights are currently stipulated for these), and single horse 150kg and single pony 90kg, again with no separate international weight set for these.

Since wire spokes and pneumatic tyres are not permitted, it is hardly possible to build a single pony vehicle which is strong enough for the job and weighs less than 90kg and most traditional carts for single horses weigh at least 150kg. The same carts can be used for tandems with some ballast. Many four-wheeled vehicles are, however, lighter than these specified weights and, in the case of horse teams, to an extent which cannot reasonably be adjusted by ballast.

The rules allow a separate vehicle to be used for the marathon in all classes, and competitors who bring two separate ones to trials are concerned mainly with producing a more beautiful one for presentation and dressage but not risking it on a marathon, except in the case of horse teams where the weight difference of 200kg or more may be significant. The standard track width for the obstacle competition is a new rule for 1985 and this may result in more drivers using two vehicles in all classes so as to benefit from a narrower one in the marathon.

Two-wheeled vehicles for single horses and horse tandems built to

stand the rigours of a marathon course within the weight limit are likely
to cost from £800 to £1,500. A recent innovation which confers some
practical advantage is for a step to be fitted on the back on which the
groom may stand so as to be more helpful in maintaining the stability
of the cart and able to get down and help more quickly in an emergency.
This means that the seat must be adjustable for balance and adds somewhat to the cost. The arrangement normally increases the weight too
much for it to be worth while for pony carts.

Four-wheeled marathon vehicles, which have picked up the un-
attractive sobriquet of 'battle wagons', are still undergoing a most
enterprising process of evolution. Hydraulic disc brakes, special springing with shock absorbers, and specially sprung poles whose heights
tend to remain more constant over rough ground and transmit less
strain to the forecarriage are now almost standard, as are tapered roller
bearings which enable wheels to turn more freely. In their commend-
able efforts to retain some semblance of tradition and thwart the introduction of revolutionary mechanical devices which may create serious
inequity, legislators are just about keeping pace with innovators. They

The carriage must be of robust construction to stand the rigours of the
marathon. George Pyecroft nearly through the water *(Findlay Davidson)*

were too late to ban telescopic axles which gave rise to suspicions of cheating when (until 1985) the obstacle cones were set to suit the track widths of each vehicle. Vehicles with a hinge in the middle, which are misnamed 'equirotals' and allow the box seat and forecarriage to turn as one with the rear wheels simply trailing behind and carrying virtually no weight, have also escaped a ban. These latter have not, in fact, given their owners any startling advantage, though the fact that the driver remains squarely behind his horses in sharp turns and does not have to make big rein adjustments is a help. The innovators, or progressives as opposed to the traditionalists, were too slow to introduce a locking device for their forecarriages, which would have made reining back much easier, and this arrangement was banned before it was invented. The innovations increase costs and complications, and the risk of mechanical failure, but they have added much general interest, and good will has always prevailed concerning them so that they have not created jealousy or been disallowed retrospectively.

The best guide for a layman to the mechanical and engineering considerations involved in the design of marathon vehicles is in the Duke of Edinburgh's comprehensive chapter on the subject in his book *Competition Carriage Driving*. Most drivers will, however, fight shy of the cost, if not the calculating, involved in creating their own designs and they may safely leave this to one of the four or five specialist carriage builders whose vehicles are currently proving their worth in competitions. These experts form only about ten per cent of those whose services are advertised, so a personal recommendation from at least one successful trials driver should be sought.

A very beautiful gig may gain you one extra presentation mark in a single or tandem class but, unless it is nearly as light as the weight specified for your marathon vehicle, it will not improve your dressage or cone driving. It is wrong to risk wrecking a beautiful gig on a marathon so you will have to take another cart as well to trials. This will save you some cleaning between Competitions B and C, but the motor transport involved will be more complicated and expensive. Much the same considerations apply if you are contemplating using a very beautiful phaeton for a pair, although if you already own a large horsebox the transport situation will be easier. With a team of horses in particular, or a team of ponies to a slightly lesser extent, the second beautiful carriage for Competitions A and C will be more worth while because it will be lighter than your marathon vehicle and help you to drive a better dressage test and obstacle competition. It will not add greatly to your motor transport problem because you will have to have a large horsebox and trailer or equivalent in any case.

A gig will cost between £1,000 and £1,500, or much more if it has antique value. A phaeton or dog-cart or equivalent will cost between £1,500 and £2,000 with the same proviso as to antiquity. The same vehicles for ponies may cost slightly less but only to the extent of £200 or £300.

A four-wheeled vehicle specially built for marathons will cost between £1,500 and £3,000 according to whether it is for a pony pair or a horse team, and you may well pay up to £5,000 for a special one with extra equipment and refinements. A serious trials driver will need at least one exercise cart for use at home in addition to those he takes to events. A two-wheeled cart for a single pony or horse need not cost much more than £150 to £200. It should be about the same weight as the trials vehicle and can be stripped of any embellishments to reduce it to this if necessary.

Pair drivers will need a four-wheeled exercise vehicle of similar weight to their marathon one, or a little lighter. This may cost £200 to £300. They will find it useful to keep a two-wheeled cart as well, plus the extra harness, to exercise a horse if his companion is lame, or perhaps to drive him alone to correct an incipient fault. This recommendation applies almost equally to owners of four-in-hands and to any driving stable in general.

Team drivers really need to keep a lighter four-wheeled vehicle in addition to their marathon one for use with their horses and ponies in pair harness and to save risking their best one for everyday exercise. This requirement is more important for horse teams than for pony teams because of the greater weight of the horses' marathon carriage.

Two-wheeled carts will normally fit a horse or pony which measures 5cm (2in) more or less than the height which it is ideally built for. The horse should be measured from the ground to the tug, and any cart can then be checked from the ground to the tug stop provided it is held level. The body and shafts of a two-wheeled cart can be raised up to 8cm (3in) on blocks above the springs, but a difference beyond this is not worth considering as the shafts and general proportions are likely to be wrong.

Four-wheeled carts will usually fit horses 8cm (3in) higher or lower than those they are ideally made for, but cannot be easily altered beyond these limits. The height of the rein rail and the pole head from the ground can be compared with that of the horses' croups and the points of their shoulders to assess relative sizes. The measurements will be rather more critical in the case of small ponies.

Properly built vehicles will last up to a hundred years with comparatively little maintenance.

Harness

Horses and ponies must have two sets of harness for driving trials since the marathon is inevitably hard on it as regards damage and it is unreasonable to contemplate cleaning the same set for presentation as has been used for the marathon and daily exercise. The best set, which

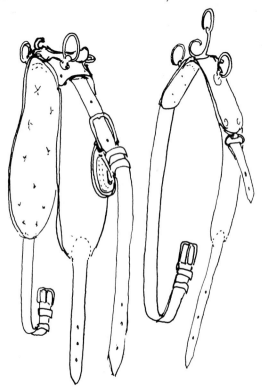

Saddle or pad for a single horse (left) and pad for the wheelers of a four-in-hand

should be used for Competitions A and C, should be leather with brass furniture and mountings; white metal mountings are not incorrect, particularly if the polished metal fittings on the vehicle and lamps are the same colour, but they are unusual and reminiscent of trade harness. Hames, kidney links, and fittings and even buckles which are subjected

129

to strain should be of steel, but brass plated, for extra strength. Black harness is slightly smarter than brown and more appropriate with a painted rather than a varnished carriage; it usually costs a little more than brown. Harness can last for well over fifty years if it is well kept, so good second-hand sets are well worth looking for at auction sales and in newspaper advertisements. The brass furniture of pre-war harness in particular seems to be of better quality than that made in recent years.

Some modern harness is made mainly of webbing and nylon and is lighter, easier to clean, and cheaper to repair than leather harness. It is also much cheaper to buy and serves very well for the marathon and for exercise at home. It necessarily incorporates breast collars rather than neck collars and these are effective provided that the total weight to be pulled is well under that of the horses which are to pull it. Harness is adjustable within a height range of about one hand (10cm) except for neck collars which must fit to within 1cm (½in) and should be worn only by the horses for which they are individually selected.

Traditional brass-mounted leather harness will cost from £150 for a set for a single small pony up to £2,000 for a set for a team of four horses, the neck collars alone being worth up to £100 each. Webbing and nylon harness with breast collars bought new will cost from £50 for a single pony set up to £500 for a specially-made set for a team of four horses.

Some spare harness is required for display in presentation and at the start of the marathon as well as for making adjustments and repairs at home, but this should not cost more than about one-tenth of the price of the equivalent full set. A full scale of appropriate single harness for driving trials is likely to cost £400 for a pony or £500 for a horse, and it is sensible to double this price for a pair or tandem and quadruple it for a team.

Accessories and Appointments

English bow-topped whips suitable for presentation and dressage will cost between £50 and £150, the higher price being for team and tandem whips. Lamps will cost between £50 and £100 a pair. An antique value, which is sometimes spurious, is often attached to these articles, particularly at auctions, but there are still a few craftsmen making new ones at realistic prices.

Grooms' liveries bought new with the coats and breeches tailor-made will probably now cost nearly £1,000 for each suit. This cost can prob-

Karen Bassett with her British spotted ponies at Bicton, 1984. These are said to be a revival of a very ancient breed *(K. G. Ettridge, Horse & Driving)*

ably be reduced to under £400 a suit by sensible second-hand buying and, since they are not necessary except for horse teams (and only optional for these), they may be regarded as the lowest priority for a limited budget.

The Complete Turnout

The cost of a complete driving turnout ready for trials but with no significant competitive form or performance record, is therefore likely to be: £1,500 for a single pony turnout, £2,000 for a single horse turnout, £3,000 for a pony tandem, £4,000 for a horse tandem, £3,750 for a pony pair, £5,000 for a horse pair, £9,000 for a pony team, and £17,000 for a horse team. Anyone who manages to put a decent turnout together for much less than this will be a hard bargainer, and a lucky one, and it will not be very out of order to pay twice as much.

131

The Cost of Keep

The cost of keeping driving horses is no different to that of keeping any others. They must, however, be kept fit and stabled throughout the summer season and cannot just be turned out in the winter, even if they are not to be kept in work or go hunting.

The annual forage bill for a horse is likely to be £600 or £700, and a small pony will eat half this amount. Shoeing and veterinary bills need be no higher for harness horses than for any others in regular work, and the latter can be covered by insurance, but repair bills are likely to be higher for driving than for riding because of the vehicles and harness.

For the same reason, there is usually rather more work connected with driving horses, particularly if they have to be turned out regularly in show condition. Two members of a family can look after a single horse or pony quite easily provided that one of them can be at home most of the time, and a pair or tandem will not be a great burden on a similar family unless a reserve horse is also kept. However, a well-organised four-in-hand plus its reserve horses needs two full-time grooms, even if the owner does most of the exercising in harness. An extra person for travelling to events is a convenience amounting almost to a necessity in any case, and someone else will usually have to be left to look after things at home.

Horseboxes and Motor Transport

The biggest expense for any trials driver, both in capital cost and overall running costs, will almost certainly be the motor transport for getting to events and the living arrangements at them. Most people should be able to get to five or six one-day club events each summer without having to stay away from home for a night and will need only the basic transport for their horses and carriages. But any more ambitious programme will prove very expensive, or very inconvenient and uncomfortable, without portable stabling, a caravan or tent, and a land-rover or car with four-wheel drive for running about as well as for inspecting the marathon course.

A land-rover with a truck body can carry a two-wheeled cart, with the shafts extending over the cab, and pull a trailer with one or two horses in it. This is an economical way of transporting a single turnout, or even possibly a tandem. It provides a runabout on arrival and needs only one driving licence holder, but the tentage and accommodation

Horse and single cart loaded in a trailer

which can be carried must be severely limited and journeys in the trailer will be slow and rather tiring for horses.

There is an enormous range of horseboxes on the market both as regards size and cost. The biggest, articulated vehicles can carry five horses in herring-bone formation, one in which they always travel very comfortably, as well as two carriages, the harness and equipment, and the framework and canvas for portable stabling which is erected along one side of the lorry. Many of these also have cooking and toilet facilities compactly fitted into them and there is plenty of room for people to sleep in them on camp beds. They can be fitted with water tanks, but

Trailer transport for a tandem

Charles Cheston, USA, with his Appaloosa pair in dressage at the Royal Windsor Show in 1984 *(Horse & Driving)*

hay usually has to be carried on roof racks. These will be very heavy lorries, up to 12m (40ft) long, and liable to bog down in soft ground, but event organisers do provide parking for them and some trials drivers do own them.

A shorter, non-articulated lorry can pull its own trailer and provide an extra 2–3m (8–10ft) of internal length for more living accommodation or storage space to carry a small car or land-rover on board. Most horseboxes can of course tow a caravan instead of their own trailer, so that if both are available, as well as a land-rover or a four-wheel-drive car, a number of combinations are possible to provide great flexibility in accordance with the length of the journey and the duration of the event. A small motor-cycle, preferably of the silent variety, can be carried on the horsebox or trailer for running about and reconnaisance. This serves well enough for a pair, tandem or single competitor.

The biggest well-equipped, custom-built horseboxes may cost up to £30,000 new, but serviceable second-hand ones may be bought for as little as £5,000. The portable stabling for five horses with the necessary fittings to attach it to the side of the horsebox will cost between £700 and £1,000, or significantly less on a 'do-it-yourself' basis. It will pay for itself in one busy year because the hire charge for temporary stabling, even when (occasionally) subsidised by the event organisers, is high at upwards of £30 per horse per night. Horses settle into their own familiar portable stabling much better than into strange boxes. They are mildly uncomfortable only in very wet or very hot weather and are not disturbed by the proximity of their human partners, although they tend to keep the latter awake at night, being invariably less sound sleepers. The inconvenience of stabling away from the showground and having to load and unload twice or even four times a day makes arrangements of this kind not worth while, even if the stabling is free.

It is better to take one's own hay than to rely on buying it on a show-

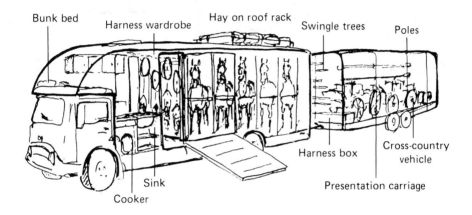

Bunk bed Harness wardrobe Hay on roof rack Swingle trees Poles

Cross-country vehicle

Harness box

Presentation carriage

Sink

Cooker

Large horsebox for five horses and two vehicles, showing living accommodation and temporary stabling erected

ground and very particular people have been known to take their own water, although this can add 750kg (15cwt) to the load even if it is carried in well-designed integral tanks. Bedding can always be bought on the showground and is only really needed in wet weather.

It is realistic to allow £1 per mile for overall travel costs for a large entourage appropriate to a team of four horses, but this can be halved for a pair and almost halved again for a single.

Administrative Planning for Trials

The problem of horses being properly rested and properly exercised must be taken into account in the planning of long journeys to driving trials. The need for them to balance themselves constantly against the sway of a moving vehicle tires them quite considerably but does not exercise them, and this effect is greatly increased if they travel in a trailer. On straight roads, such as motorways, speed does not materially increase this effect so the aim should be to travel as quickly as possible and reduce the journey time.

It is probably better not to travel for more than four hours without a halt, but the halt will be of little value unless the horses can be unloaded and have at least a twenty-minute walk and a feed on terra firma. Six hours uninterrupted travel is about the limit for horses which are to compete the next day, and if a longer journey than this is envisaged it should be broken by an overnight stop or at least one clear day should be allowed at the event before the first competition.

With all the extra work involved in preparation, and the inevitable interruption to normal stable routine which competing at a trial involves, it is all too easy to forget the need for horses to continue their regular work and exercise, and a special effort is needed to maintain this and ensure that they stay in peak condition both mentally and physically. One must usually travel to an event on the day before the first competition is to take place and it makes sense to do so early and allow time to make administrative arrangements, inspect the marathon course, and give the horses an hour's steady exercise to relieve the stiffness of travel.

It is not realistic to attempt any long exercise with the best harness immediately before or after the dressage test and its necessary warming-up period, but it is a good thing to get the horses out again for an hour in the afternoon or evening after this. Half an hour's very steady work is enough before the marathon, and no more than this is needed before the obstacle competition on the third day, after which most people travel home, even if this takes them several hours. Normal routine should, however, be resumed on the day after this and it is the sigh of relief and the break for a two- or three-day rest at this stage which disrupts the programme and results in horses being off form for their next event only nine or ten days later.

The Total Bill

People who are really interested in costs may probably conclude that the whole establishment for a top-class turnout for a four-horse team can cost up to £75,000 in capital and up to £20,000 a year in running costs. That for a single pony kept on the most economical lines but capable of winning a national championship could cost £5,000 in capital, including the motor transport, and £1,500 a year to run.

8
Judges and Officials

'It's only the referee!'

Driving trials are labour-intensive activities which need at least as many people to run them as those who compete in them. The number of judges, officials and other workers required is seldom less than a hundred and sometimes nearly two hundred. This requirement could be reduced by a radical revision of the rules but, to the extent that it involves the participation of many enthusiastic helpers who cannot afford to compete themselves, it maintains the active interest of a wide range of supporters from the whole horse world and justifies the trouble which organisers have to take to assemble them.

The Judges

The number of fully-qualified judges required is dictated by the number of entries, the number of classes into which they are divided, and the number of dressage arenas available. At World and European Championships there is usually only one class, that for which the Championship is designated, so it is judged by one ground jury of five members and an appeal jury of three members, who may also judge the presentation if required.

At national events there may be a hundred or more entries divided into eight classes so that if Competition A, presentation and dressage, is to be completed in one day, four juries of three members each must be engaged to judge this in three separate arenas. A ground jury of at least three judges is required to supervise and judge the marathon and, although two are enough to judge the obstacle competition as regards its scoring, three should be watching it in case of a split decision. Thus more than twelve judges may be needed if the timetable requires any of the three competitions to overlap, but an appeal jury can normally be appointed from among those who are not involved in decisions about which appeals may be made.

Judges are appointed by recommendation from a member of the Driving Trials Committee of the British Horse Society to the whole committee, and must serve a period of probation. They must bring to their task knowledge, integrity and availability. It is a great advantage for them to have some experience of judging ridden dressage and, although they will not be required to demonstrate this capability, they should be able to drive competently themselves.

They must know the relevant dressage test thoroughly by heart, including the requirements to be judged for each movement, and they must know all the special words and phrases used in dressage so that their remarks will be meaningful and concise. They must also have 'an eye for a horse' to the extent of being able to recognise instantly any lameness at the trot since, although only the president of a jury is required to take action about this, the freedom and regularity of the horses' paces is a constant criterion and even a hint of unlevelness will affect it and should influence the scoring accordingly.

The judging of of presentation can be learned from a book and a few sessions under a good tutor, and anyone who has passed the proficiency tests of the British Driving Society will have no difficulty with this. Judicial decisions about the marathon require a thorough understanding of the rule book and the correct interpretation of the rules in it, but no judge is expected to know all these by heart since he will have time to refer to them. The rules for the obstacle competition must, however, be learned by heart since instant decisions are nearly always required.

A good judge should acquire a working knowledge of the rules for ridden horse trials and show jumping and of the general regulations of the International Equestrian Federation, since he is always liable to encounter problems not fully covered by the more recent driving trials rules which derive from these.

The Appeal Jury

The appeal jury, or appeal committee, of three people is appointed by the same authority as the ground jury to hear appeals against decisions of the ground jury in certain circumstances and to decide some considerations referred directly to it by the ground jury as being beyond their immediate competence.

Competitors have the right of appeal against decisions of the ground jury if they consider that these have been based on misinterpretations of the rules or if they feel that penalties awarded, not being mandatory ones or penalty points related to timing or a judicial opinion, are unduly severe. In practice, this means that it is pointless, and will be expensive because the deposit of £20 will be lost, to appeal against a score in presentation or dressage, mandatory penalty points for a rule infringement, elimination for taking a wrong course or exceeding the time limit in the marathon, or elimination for a third refusal in the obstacle competition. It may, however, be worth appealing against disqualification or elimination if this is awarded for an infringement for which no set penalty, or a lesser penalty, is specified in the rules.

Contrary to the suspicions of some competitors, the ground jury will usually try to find in their favour or be as lenient as possible in their award of penalties, always provided that they must consider the situation as regards all the other competitors who, being innocent of the infringement in question, are entitled to benefit accordingly.

The rules are still indefinite about the differences between disqualification, elimination, withdrawal and retirement but these are fairly obvious to anyone with knowledge of other competitive sports whose rules are longer established. A competitor will normally be disqualified if he fails to comply with any of the conditions imposed for a specific event or the trials in general, and particularly if this failure gives him an advantage, as in the matter of weight or measurements. He is also likely to be disqualified if he deliberately breaks a rule and thereby gains an advantage, or ignores a safety regulation and puts himself or other people at risk. Being disqualified he ceases to take part in the event, cannot be rewarded or classified for any competition in it which he may have already completed, and may incur further disciplinary action.

A competitor will always be eliminated if he takes the wrong course and thereby fails to undergo the same test as his rivals, and it will normally be assumed that he has done this inadvertently and not deliberately. He will also be eliminated if he exceeds a time limit, as in a marathon obstacle, and thereby threatens to delay the competition and to amass a score of penalties out of proportion to those of the other competitors. By a kindly provision of the rules he is debited with the score of the lowest placed competitor in the competition plus 25 per cent but is allowed to count his score and win any prize for either of the other two competitions; but he may not be classified above any uneliminated competitor for the whole event.

A competitor may withdraw in certain circumstances from one or two of the three competitions of an event before the start of it but still compete *hors concours* in the remaining ones, or he may be ordered to withdraw by a judge, usually on veterinary advice or because his vehicle has been damaged and cannot safely proceed, either before or during a competition. He may retire at his own discretion during any competition without being required to give any reason for doing so. A competitor who retires from one competition will be treated for scoring and final classification in the same way as one who is eliminated but must be classified below those who are eliminated in the final order for the event. A competitor who withdraws may count his score for any competition before the one from which he withdraws but may not compete in any subsequent one, other than *hors concours*, so cannot figure in the final classification. A judge will normally invite a competitor to retire rather than order him to withdraw if this action becomes necessary, thus enabling him to compete in the third competition if he has a reserve horse.

The Technical Delegate

To justify his sonorous title this functionary must inspect and approve the dressage arenas, the marathon course and its obstacles, and the obstacle competition course. He must also ensure that the obstacle judges, referees and timekeepers are fully briefed and understand their duties and, unless he is of a very trusting disposition, he will brief them himself. He is appointed, for each event, by the Driving Trials Committee of the British Horse Society for all national trials held in Great Britain, and by the Driving Committee of the International Equestrian Federation for all international championships.

He is responsible to the committee which appoints him and thus to its parent organisation — the national federation concerned or the International Equestrian Federation — for seeing that the courses are fair for all competitors and that drivers with local knowledge do not have an obvious advantage over those who are visiting the locality for the first time. He must also ensure that the rules and regulations are complied with and that the technical arrangements for the running of the event, including veterinary facilities, are satisfactory. These will include the scoring and the posting of the results for each competition as well as the publication of the starting times for them.

The technical delegate has no judicial function to perform and must not allow himself to be drawn into any arguments or objections about decisions of the ground jury or appeal jury. He continues to be responsible for supervising the technical conduct of the event even after he has approved the arrangements and signified this to the president of the ground jury.

At international championships and official international driving events (Concours d'Attelage Internationale Officiel — CAIO) he is also responsible to the International Equestrian Federation for approving all the administrative arrangements which may affect the competitors, including the stabling and the accommodation for drivers and grooms and their travel and transport requirements. He is not expected to undertake this extra administrative responsibility at national trials where, in Britain, he performs the same duties as the British Horse Society steward does at ridden horse trials.

To do his job properly the technical delegate will usually have to make one or two preliminary visits to the site of an event well before it is due to take place. In particular, he can save the organisers trouble and expense by inspecting and approving the layout of the marathon course and the design of its obstacles before any manual work is done on them and posts are actually driven into the ground.

There is a natural tendency for inexperienced organisers to rely too much on a technical delegate to the extent of treating him as the technical director of their event. The man in question will wish to be friendly and helpful and may succumb to the temptation of introducing ideas and innovations of his own into the marathon course and the general arrangements. This is undesirable in that he may tend to defend them against criticism from the competitors or the jury instead of inspecting them objectively. He has considerable authority delegated to him but must use this with discretion and avoid assuming autocratic powers.

The Obstacle Judges

Three or four obstacle judges are needed to look after each of the eight obstacles in a full marathon course, and this does not include relief judges for a long day. The reason is that two people are usually required to time the drivers between entry and exit through an obstacle which may be more than 20m long. This timing is critical and must be recorded meticulously to the nearest second. On a few recent occasions when electronic-beam timing, which either operates accurately or not at all, has been used to time individual obstacles, it has proved that variations in human reaction time have produced disturbingly inconsistent results. The cost of providing this equipment for all marathon obstacles at a national, or even international, event is still so prohibitive that the human eye must be relied upon for the foreseeable future and the task, though tedious at twelve or fifteen times an hour over an eight-hour day, is crucially demanding.

A third member of each obstacle judging team is needed to ensure that drivers take the correct course through the obstacle, and the inevitable arguments which arise when they are deemed not to have done so, and are eliminated accordingly, are best resolved by reference to a drawing of the actual course taken which this judge must make. A fourth member must stand by to stop an oncoming competitor at a suitable distance before the obstacle if the previous competitor is still struggling in it; and unless the delayed driver has a referee with him, the time that he is held up must be accurately recorded to be credited to him.

Obstacle judges are required to give a factual account of the performance of each competitor through their obstacle, in theory to the ground jury but in practice to the scorers. They are not expected to make judicial decisions except when a competitor is still in the obstacle after the statutory time limit of five minutes when they must tell him that he is eliminated and see that he leaves it. It is a help if they can make their reports precisely by radio after each driver has negotiated their obstacle, but they must record the facts in writing as well.

B.H.S. 1983
INTERNATIONAL AND
NATIONAL
1st March 1983

HORSE DRIVING TRIALS
INSTRUCTIONS FOR OBSTACLE JUDGES

1. You will receive:
    (a) Obstacle Judges' Book
    (b) Stopwatches (2) (or one double digital clock)
    (c) Whistle
    (d) Sketch of your Obstacle for each Competitor

2. On receiving your Obstacle Judges' Book place the cardboard under each blue copy sheet. Write Judge's name, class number, sheet number, and obstacle number on each sheet. If the competitor has negotiated the obstacle without fault enter only the time taken in the last column. Indicate any faults in the obstacle by ticking the relevant column. If you consider the competitor eliminated indicate so in the relevant column and, if necessary give further details on the back of the sheet.

3. Competitor is under your jurisdiction from entering the penalty zone until leaving it after negotiating the obstacle correctly.

4. Penalties in the obstacle are as follows:–

Driver putting down his whip at any time	20
One Groom dismounting (foot on ground)	10
Second Groom dismounting (i.e. two grooms dismounting = 20 penalties)	10
Driver dismounting (additional to the grooms)	30
Turning over (this includes any other penalties incurred)	60
Any part of the team or vehicle leaving the penalty zone before completing the obstacle	20
Disconnecting and leading the leaders separately through any part of the obstacle	Elimination

144

Failure to pass through one of the gates	Elimination
Knocking down collapsible elements — each gateway or part thereof	10

5. Treat penalty zone line as start and finish for timing. Record total time through obstacle in the last column. Take the time from the moment the first part of the turnout enters the zone to the moment the first part leaves the zone.

6. Ensure that the Competitor passes through each element of the obstacle in the sequence shown, unless it is a "Take your own line" obstacle. But remember that the competitor is allowed to go through an element again. For instance, he must go through A correctly before going through B but may go through A again in either direction and so on. In a "Take your own line" obstacle check that the competitor has passed through each element. Tick each element on the sketch as the competitor goes through. Remember that he can go through any gate again in either direction once he has negotiated it correctly.

7. After the time limit of 5 minutes has expired, blow two blasts on the whistle, and see that the competitor leaves the obstacle immediately.

8. Obstacle Judges are requested to remain within easy reach of the public address system until officially released by the President of the Jury or his Representative.

9. Watches may only be used by the appointed Obstacle Judge or his Assistant. Under no circumstances may children be allowed to use the watch.

N.B. If you have any trouble with your stopwatch send a message to control as soon as possible and the official time keeper will come to see you.

The Referees

A referee accompanies each competitor in horse and pony team classes and horse pair classes, but not pony pair, tandem or single classes because of the weight. He is required to report any errors of course, except in obstacles where the obstacle judges take over, any diversions from it which involve missing a compulsory turning flag, and any breaks of pace. He must also note and report other infringements of the rules about which he will be briefed before starting. He must record the time taken for each section in case the ground timekeeping fails, as well as any time for which his competitor is held up or delayed other than through his own fault, so that this may be credited to the driver in the scoring.

Despite some risk of injury which is inseparable from it, this is a popular job which is much sought after and ought, as far as possible, to be awarded by organisers to helpers who have served their apprenticeship in the less glamorous areas of the voluntary structure. The referee is required to wear a bowler hat or hard hat to lessen the risk of injury and to serve as an easily identifiable mark of his office. He will be expected to report to the technical delegate for briefing well before the start of the marathon; quite often on the day before, and will normally be taken round the course and shown the turning flags and other salient features.

Like obstacle judges, referees report facts, including times recorded on the clocks issued to them, and do not make judicial decisions. They report these to a member of the ground jury at the finish of the marathon and generally leave the interpretations to him, save only that they must form an opinion about breaks of pace.

The criterion for awarding penalties for breaks of pace is whether or not they are considered to have gained an advantage for the competitor concerned. Because assessments about this varied so widely, an instruction was issued in 1982 that any break of pace lasting less than five seconds should not be counted. As a rule of thumb this works well but referees must count the seconds and not take their eyes off the horses to refer to a watch. 'One thousand and one' etc counted to oneself quite slowly equates with the passage of seconds and a penalty point should be scored every time a multiple of five is reached.

Referees must have some knowledge and experience of horses so that they can identify breaks of pace with certainty from a viewpoint above and behind the horses concerned. They should be fairly active so as to be able to look after themselves if the carriage overturns and be helpful in this and similar emergencies. There is an understandable tendency for a referee to become a partisan of his competitor, who will obviously encourage this. This tendency must be sternly but politely resisted and referees must remain strictly impartial, particularly if they are required to give evidence to the ground jury about incidents involving objections or disputed decisions.

B.H.S. 1983
INTERNATIONAL AND
NATIONAL
1st March 1983

HORSE DRIVING TRIALS
INSTRUCTIONS FOR REFEREES

1. Referees must sit alongside the driver.

2. The Referee will be issued with

    (a) Clipboard
    (b) Pink or white referees' card
    (c) Two stopwatches (or one double digital clock)
    (d) Plan of course
    (e) Referees' Instruction sheet
    (f) Pencils

3. He must record on his card the following:–

    (a) Any deviation from the course, i.e. if a numbered flag has not been passed on the correct side or in the correct sequence.

    (b) Any break of pace, faster or slower, only one horse need break. He must record each period of 5 seconds that the break of pace continues. At the end of the marathon he should inform the debriefing judge of the incidents. The referee must acquaint himself with any places that have been marked by the Technical Delegate allowing a different pace to that stipulated for the Section.

    (c) Any time taken by a competitor for a halt — other than the compulsory halts — and the reason for such halts. (No halts are allowed other than for an accident or repair to harness or vehicles.)

    (d) Grooms dismounting in Sections B (Walk) or D (Walk). For dismounting in either of these sections, the referee must award 20 penalty marks on each occasion. Grooms dismounting in other sections (except the penalty zone, which will be penalised by the Obstacle Judge) will not be penalised.

    (e) Cantering or trotting of the whole turnout in a Walk Section (Sections B and D). The penalty is elimination, but such incidents must be reported to the President of the Jury who will confirm the penalty.

4. The Referee must use the two stopwatches (or the double digital clock) handed to him, one to record the time taken on each section and one to record any delays or stops that may occur, in particular any hold-ups

147

before entering the penalty zone of an obstacle. Although Referees' Times are only used as a check against the Official Time Keeper's they are nevertheless important.

5. No other person than the driver may hold the whip, or reins from the box or use the brake. However, should a competitor lose, break or drop his whip for any reason, a groom or passenger may pick it up and hand it to him or pass the spare whip without penalty unless this occurs in a Walk Section in which case Dismounting will be penalised 20 penalty marks. (Should this occur in a penalty zone the Obstacle Judge will award any penalties incurred.)

6. The Referee must report any outside assistance, this includes being followed or accompanied by any vehicle, bicycle, pedestrian or horseman (other than an official), advice or directions from friends as to conditions of going, time and distances, having someone at an obstacle to encourage or assist competitor or horses by any means whatsoever. (Help at the compulsory halts or in case of an accident is not considered outside assistance.) Try to identify who gave advice and stop them.

7. The Referee must report any deliberate acts of cruelty such as excessive use of the whip or excessive pressing of the exhausted horses. He must warn the competitor immediately and report such acts to the appointed Judge at the first halt after the incident.

8. The Referee must ensure that if his competitor is caught up, the competitor following should be allowed to pass. The Referee must record any delays caused in this way.

9. Although not their primary duty, the Referees are asked to see that their competitor arrives at the start on time.

10. Referees must report to the Judge immediately on the finish of the Marathon and must remain within easy reach of the public address system until officially released by the President of the Jury or his representative.

There is an understandable temptation for a Referee to become partisan. He should resist this temptation and remain strictly impartial both during the marathon and the hearing of any objection or enquiry which may be held after it.

The Timekeepers

A timekeeper is required at the start and finish of each marathon section. He or she needs a companion to provide temporary relief during a long day and because the green cards carried by competitors must be collected, filled in with the times, and returned to the competitor at each start and finish at the same time as the white master time-sheet is filled in. For speed and extra efficiency timekeepers may also be provided with a radio through which the times they have recorded may be transmitted verbally to the scorers.

The electronic digital clocks owned by the Driving Trials Group of the British Horse Society are tamper-proof, virtually foolproof, and dead accurate to the extent that they either stop or go quite wrong or keep exact time. With only one external control, which freezes the digital display so that it can be read unhurriedly and recorded before a second pressure releases the freeze and shows the correct time again, these clocks are almost incapable of inaccuracy provided that they are synchronised with one another when they are first started. This job, which is the ultimate responsibility of the technical delegate, is usually delegated to a chief timekeeper who may brief all the timekeepers and must travel constantly between them to supervise their duties and ensure that their clocks remain synchronised.

The Scorers

The calculating and recording of the scores for Competitions A and C is only a matter of simple arithmetic, but for Competition B, the marathon, the requirement is more complex. Up to thirty separate calculations and entries may have to be made and entered on the score-sheet for each competitor, and unless most of the working is shown innumerable queries are likely to result. This needs a team of at least three people with an experienced leader who must ensure that all figures are checked at least once before they are posted.

It is helpful for the scorers to be in radio contact with the timekeepers and obstacle judges so that they can receive results instantly and check queries verbally, but this arrangement really requires two extra people to answer on the two radio sets which will be involved.

The scorers need fairly isolated weather-proof accommodation near the finish of the marathon and this must be out of bounds to everyone else except the president of the jury and the technical delegate. It is reasonable for these two officials to query suspected mistakes in arithmetic directly with the scorers and to authorise any corrections, but no other complainants should be allowed to approach them.

Extra people are required to post the results on the main score-board and a second one in the stable area and, since these must be displayed complete for each class for half an hour before they are confirmed to allow time for any objections to be made, the speed and accuracy with which the scorers do their work plays a vital part in the timing and the smooth running of an event.

The Veterinary Officials

In addition to the veterinary cover which must be provided throughout the duration of an event for the treatment of sick or injured horses, the rules specify the appointment of a veterinary officer to carry out a mandatory examination when the horses arrive at the event and an inspection of all horses at the compulsory halt at the end of Section D of the marathon and before Competition C. At championships and official international events, a veterinary commission of three members must be appointed to be responsible for these checks and to conduct a further inspection before Competition A and a further examination immediately after Competition B.

Veterinary officials effectively advise the ground jury who order the withdrawal or compulsory retirement of horses which are not passed as fit. Competitors have no right of appeal against decisions made on veterinary grounds.

The veterinary commission may also be required to conduct dope tests at important championships. The analysis of the samples taken is a very expensive procedure and, in a contest in which absolute speed is not called for and tranquillising drugs are liable to be embarrassingly uncertain in their effects, doping is not likely to be resorted to. However, there must always be a temptation for drivers, particularly of four-horse teams, to resort to pain-killing drugs to mask the symptoms of lameness and keep their best horses in action, and regular monitoring of this possibility is the only positive safeguard against such an undesirable practice.

150

The Judges' Writers

The ladies — they are nearly always ladies — who volunteer to write for dressage judges do a vital job which deserves more recognition than it gets, because unless they do it well their judges are liable to become muddled and may fail to judge fairly. They will usually spend much more time looking at their papers than at the tests for which they are recording scores and are not required to know or study the tests or expected to become unduly interested in them. Because the individual movements last longer in driven than in ridden dressage, judges' comments are often comparatively fuller and longer; and indeed it is right that they should be when the drivers concerned are novices and can benefit from advice.

Judges are expected to tell their writers exactly what to write and to announce the score for each movement at the end of each comment about it so that the writer will automatically then continue to the next movement on the sheet without the need for any other talk. A writer must never talk to a judge between the time that a competitor enters the arena and the time that his score-sheet is signed by the judge, because an interruption to his concentration cannot be allowed. If a judge's comment is confusing or too long for the column on the score-sheet a writer may legitimately clarify or condense it without consulting the judge, provided that she is certain of the mark given. She must, however, tell the judge at once if she becomes uncertain about the actual movement she is recording, because a mistake made in this respect will be very difficult to put right afterwards.

The Course Builder

The competent execution of the course builder's job is vital to the success of a driving trial. The same person may design and build both the marathon course with its obstacles and the obstacle competition course, and in this case he will probably lay out the dressage arenas as well. Alternatively, a separate course builder may be engaged for the marathon course and the obstacle competition course, and a steward may take the responsibility for laying out the dressage arenas. Exceptionally, two people may share responsibility for designing and building a marathon course, and this arrangement works well when one of them lives locally and knows the area well and the other has experience of building marathon obstacles.

151

The task of laying out a good marathon course involves a careful study of the available ground to make the best use of it in terms of providing good going, even in wet weather, and a logical route which is easy to follow from a map and free of other traffic.

Section A may include metalled roads; Sections B and D, the walk phases, may be entirely over metalled roads and must be on flat, level, firm ground; Sections C and E should be mainly on good turf, but may include some sand tracks; horses should not be asked to trot fast on hard roads.

Sensible signing is essential for a good marathon route, and the more so if the course has to double back on itself, to fit the necessary length into a restricted area, rather than run from point to point. Although the present rules provide for all drivers to be able to make a reconnaissance of the course, this is a time-consuming procedure which can churn the track up badly in wet weather and course designers should aim in future to sign routes so efficiently that they can be driven without any inspection. The way to achieve this is to put up more direction signs than seem to be necessary, with duplicates before turns and confidence signs just after them and on straight stretches where drivers may need reassurance. The international rules specify yellow direction signs for all sections but it is helpful, and surely permissible, to use different coloured ones for different sections if there is any question of tracks crossing or overlapping one another.

The designing and building of marathon obstacles is still in its rather protracted infancy and there is scope for its development and improvement in terms of the ingenuity of its practitioners as well as the precision of their measurements. There is a thin dividing line between the easy and the impossible as regards the space required for horses to turn a carriage through 180 degrees or more and this of course varies according to the number of horses pulling it and the gradients involved. Rules and recommendations about minimum widths and turning circles have generally proved restricting to the development of obstacle building by making straightforward manoeuvres too easy and forcing designers to incorporate extra complications.

The ultimate in tight turns is generally conceded to have been reached in the World Championships in England in 1980 and the ultimate in steep hills in those in Hungary in 1984. There does not seem to be any reasonable third dimension which can be incorporated, and future development will probably depend on combining these two demands in carefully calculated proportions. Even in World and European Championships, in which only four-horse teams driven by highly competent coachmen have been engaged, no more than two-thirds of the obstacles have so far proved to be really satisfactory. The problem is further complicated in national events in that singles, pairs and tandems have also to be catered for and cost normally prohibits the building of separate sets of obstacles. The requirement to test the best competitors without destroying the worst ones creates extra difficulty in national and regional trials in which the standard of skill varies so widely.

It is a well-established fact, which adds considerably to the fascination of his task, that no course builder can yet accurately predict the effect which his obstacles will have until several competitors have actually driven through them. This suggests that we still have a long way to go before reaching a real understanding of the problems involved and, meanwhile, speculation adds an extra interest about this at every event. It is not likely to be resolved in advance by the obvious expedient of testing the obstacles by driving a team of horses through them because drivers and horses of high enough standard to make the test effective are almost always entered for the event.

A course builder who knows the ground well and has plenty of practical experience of designing obstacles, or two people who possess this knowledge and experience between them, can make all the difference to the success or failure of a driving trial. Plenty of solid posts and rails, some hole-boring and even digging equipment, and manual labour are required and, in a sport which is still almost entirely amateur, undue economies in respect of these essential requirements are liable to be false ones.

The Stewards

Good stewarding is the key to the successful running of all competitive activities, and no more so than in the running of horse driving trials. Stewards must be available for any preliminary conferences before the event and must arrive punctually and be prepared to stay later at it than they may have anticipated. They will be particularly valuable if they are willing to do the same job at the same event each year, and the experience and knowledge which they will gain of their special responsibilities and most of the competitors whom they will be looking after will be invaluable in overcoming the problems which inevitably arise at even the best organised trials.

A chief steward is required to co-ordinate all the duties involved and to ensure that all of them are covered, and he should normally be a member of the organising committee and concerned with the planning of the event.

A stable manager with one or two assistants will be needed for trials which are to take place over more than one day or if many competitors are likely to arrive the day before.

At least two stewards are required for each dressage arena and a further two are needed to assemble competitors for presentation and to send them on to the dressage rings in case their published timetables cannot be adhered to.

There should be two stewards at the start of the marathon, one at the start of each section of it, and, ideally, an extra one at each compulsory halt. There must be a steward at the finish of the marathon, and another one with an assistant to weigh the vehicles if the weighbridge is in operation.

For Competition C, the obstacle competition, two collecting-ring stewards are required, and two, four, or even six stewards must work in pairs in the ring under the directions of the course builder to reset any cones which become displaced.

Mobile stewards are needed to collect time- and score-sheets from the marathon course, and often from the dressage arenas as well. It is a pleasant tradition for mounted members of the Pony Club to undertake this task but it is a slow method and not very practical in wet weather, considering the size of the area over which driving trials take place. Mounted stewards are however very useful for crowd control if a large number of spectators is expected on the marathon course.

If enough volunteers are available, it is useful though not essential for stewards to be appointed to look after the judges, the veterinary officials and the scorers. Their duties cannot be specified but are likely to be manifold.

Stewards, and many other officials, often need to be able to exercise courteous authority. Their appointment invests them with this, and a bowler hat, as a universally recognised badge of office, serves to identify them easily where their duties make this desirable. However, real authority stems from knowledge and ability, and helpers who can acquire the right experience by offering their services at trials all over the country, and possibly providing their own caravan accommodation, will be making a great contribution to the development of the sport by establishing a corps of experts to run it.

9
Organisation and Administration

'What do you mean, am I driving that one?'

The Area and Ground

A three-day driving trial with a full five-section marathon needs at least two thousand acres of land to contain its operations. This land, if not privately owned, must be subject to the control of the organisers to the extent of their being permitted to regulate traffic flow and public access. The organisers themselves will need full access for several months before the event to lay out the marathon course and build its obstacles. They may need to impose some restrictions on the use of the land by other people, if only to preserve the surface of the tracks and prevent interference with the markers and any other apparatus.

The Dressage Arenas

An essential requirement within this area is enough suitable ground for a dressage arena; or for two or three arenas if enough entries are to be taken to warrant extra ones. The more advanced ten-minute dressage tests can be judged at the rate of five per hour and the simpler five-minute tests at eight per hour in the 100x40m arena and nine per hour in the 80x40m one. Thus entries in excess of fifty require extra arenas or extra days. The main dressage arena needs a total area (including its surrounds) of 120x60m, and a smaller one can be fitted in to 100x60m. The main arena should be larger (120x70m) if the obstacle competition is to be held in it as well as the dressage. The ground for dressage arenas must be flat and level with no gradients; this latter requirement is more important for driven dressage than for its ridden counterpart. Their surfaces should be no rougher than that of an average racecourse with a three to four inch growth of grass into which the centre line and centre markers may be permanently mown. Firm turf is the only suitable surface for driven dressage. Sand and cinder surfaces have been tried and found to offer too much resistance to carriage wheels and, as a last resort, gravel as for a carriage drive or parade ground is probably the only possible substitute discovered to date.

It is inconvenient and causes extra administrative problems if the second dressage arena cannot be reasonably close to the first one, but they should be at least 30m apart from each other to avoid mutual distractions. An area of about one acre adjoining the dressage arenas is required for a collecting ring and for the judging of presentation, and this should if possible be within 200m of the secretary's office and the general administration area of the trials. A practice area should be within sight of the dressage arenas and this need not be very flat or level but must be as big as possible and no smaller than ten acres.

The Main Ring

The main ring for the trials invariably has the obstacle competition course set out in it and must be not less than 120x70m to suit this requirement. It will need a one-acre collecting ring adjoining it and should, ideally, be within sight of the practice area. The usual plan is for one of the dressage arenas to be laid out in this ring; or two if it is big enough. This makes a compact, convenient central focus for the trials and is the obvious arrangement when a completely level amphitheatre,

Presentation of prizes in the main ring of Aachen Show, the biggest horse show in Europe, and where the Duke of Edinburgh got his inspiration to establish driving trials internationally. German champion Bernd Duen heads the line up *(Findlay Davidson)*

artificial or natural, is available.

The need to keep the available space entirely free for the dressage arenas, however, precludes the building of any massively constructed obstacles on it, whether permanent or semi-permanent. It is often more sensible to devote the main ring to a really well-designed obstacle course, together with any other ring attractions which may be fitted into it, and to site the dressage arenas separately from it but still within reach of spectators.

The obstacle competition course is generally more interesting and spectacular if it incorporates some slopes and different levels and the last marathon obstacle can sometimes be constructed in it to good effect. Topography will usually dictate the layout in this respect, but it is not necessary for Competitions A and C both to be held in the same arena; and the comparatively few spectators who are really keen on watching driven dressage will welcome the opportunity to see it in more secluded rings round which they will be able to park their cars.

Veteran former British National Champion Coupie Brown, Chairman of the Scottish branch of the British Driving Society, with his Welsh Cob Glyn negotiating the steep bank below the walls of Lowther Castle. This event is the biggest one in Britain each year *(K. G. Ettridge, Horse & Driving)*

The Marathon Course

From the point of view of spectators, and for ease of administration, the best general layout for a marathon course is one in which the start and finish of the whole course are close to each other, and in or near the main ring and the secretarial centre of the event. It also helps administration and sustains interest if some or all of the other sections can start and finish in this area.

This arrangement is normally possible, at least in part, when the main ring is located near the centre of a big estate with parkland surrounding or adjoining it so that each section can be routed out from the centre in a big loop to a different point of the compass. It is likely to provide the additional advantage of enabling the obstacles in Section E of the marathon to be sited near the main ring and within spectators' walking distance from the car parks. This can often be contrived by having half the obstacles sited at the beginning of the section and the other half at the end of it so that they can all be seen in a walk of about a mile and are conveniently grouped for any repairs which may be necessary.

However desirable a layout of this kind may be, the need for marathon obstacles to be interesting, challenging, as innovative as possible, and of reasonably natural appearance must not be subordinated to it. They should not all be built on flat, featureless parkland if the track of Section E can be routed through a more appropriate landscape further away from the centre of operations. Water as well as hilly ground is a valuable attribute and it is well worth while establishing a special car park for spectators close to any more distant obstacles.

The Stable Area

An area of about five acres is needed for horseboxes and competitors' own caravans and portable stabling. This can be much smaller for a one-day event, for which most competitors will not need to stay overnight, but should be unrestricted for a two- or three-day event. Good firm ground, with at least one road to and through it, is essential for this, and tractors should be available to tow vehicles on and off it in case of wet weather. Trees for shade will be much appreciated and water must be laid on to the site even for a one-day trial.

For a two- or three-day event a stable manager with an assistant should be appointed to live in a caravan office on the site. He or she

159

should be able to sell limited quantities of hay to the few competitors who do not bring their own, and some straw will also be needed in very wet weather.

The normal ambulance service and a doctor, vet and farrier appointed for the trials should be on call through this office for the whole duration of the event and the afternoon and night before it, and a coin-box telephone should also be provided at it. A delivery of milk and newspapers each morning is always much appreciated. This area should be as close as possible to the main ring and administrative centre of the trials, and certainly not more than half a mile from it, but preferably well away from the public car parks.

Most British competitors now bring their own portable stabling to driving trials but organisers may have to arrange stabling for a few of them. Commercial temporary stabling erected on the site is nowadays very expensive at £40 or more for each box, and organisers cannot be expected to provide this free or even to subsidise it.

Stabling in nearby farms and yards can usually be arranged at the expense of competitors who want it, and normally at their own risk, but to be reasonably convenient for them it needs to be within two miles of the centre of the event so that the necessity of loading and unloading at least twice each day is avoided. For a one-day event, stabling can be arranged further away since it can be regarded more as an overnight staging place.

The Offices

The secretary's office is the administrative centre of a driving trial, and the siting, size, staffing and facilities available in it are crucial to the successful running of the event. It should be divided into two separate departments, one to serve spectators, trade stand exhibitors, the treasurer's requirements, and the public in general, and the other to serve competitors and officials for the trials and be, in effect, the Trials Office.

A marquee with a dividing partition is quite suitable but cannot provide overnight security for valuables and can be uncomfortable in very bad weather. Two large caravans or 'portakabins' positioned next to each other may be rather better if they can be hired at comparable cost. They have the additional advantage of tending to be slightly less accessible for casual visitors. These cannot, in courtesy, be excluded but they are a nuisance particularly when their main concern is to shelter from rain.

One main-line telephone between the two departments is essential but two, with separate lines, are a luxury. It is a great boon to have electricity laid on, and an electric copying machine will save much time and labour, particularly in the preparation of the detailed time-sheets which competitors expect to receive individually for all three competitions, and the speedy duplication of results.

The ideal, if rather lavish, staffing is a secretary and two assistants for each department and it is a great help to have one or two sensible children available to take messages which cannot be transmitted by telephone or radio.

The scorers must be separately accommodated in a caravan rather than a tent. This should be sited primarily at the finish of the marathon course, but have an alternative location near the dressage arenas if these are not in the same area and provided that it can be moved.

The announcer/commentator should normally function from a special commentary box or vehicle overlooking the main ring and containing the public address equipment. This will double as the judges' box for Competition C, the obstacle competition, and should be sited accordingly. It needs to be big enough to contain at least two judges as well as the timekeeper, scorer and commentator to serve this purpose.

This box is also normally the control for the administrative radio net and the commentator needs an assistant for most of the time to help him with his multiple responsibilities. The commentary box should be on the internal telephone network and if there is not this facility, it should have direct lines to the secretary's office, the stable manager's office and the scorers.

It may be desirable to establish one or more extra commentary points to cover the marathon, each with their separate public address systems. When this is done the commentators in them can keep an ear on the radio nets of the timekeepers and obstacle judges, as well as on the administrative one, in order to be able to keep spectators in their areas informed of the general progress of the competition.

The director of a big event will need a tent or caravan of his own close to the secretary's office but can probably share this with the chief steward and use it primarily to brief and confer with the stewards and other administrative workers.

The judges and the appeal jury also need a separate caravan which they and the technical delegate can use to hear objections and appeals and to debrief referees in bad weather. This should be sited primarily at the finish of the marathon, close to the scorers, but should ideally be

161

moved to the dressage arenas and the main ring for the other competitions if these locations are at all distant from one another.

Communications

Besides the radio nets for the marathon timekeepers and obstacle judges which are referred to in Chapter 8, it is highly desirable to have a third administrative net working on a third separate frequency. The technical provision of this has recently become comparatively easy provided that some prior attention is given to it. Confusion and jamming inevitably result if more than ten amateurs all want to speak as outstations on this net, but only cost restricts the number of radios which may be used to listen out on it. Some accepted radio discipline is therefore required if this net is to operate effectively and cover all the people whose duties may require them to be in contact on it, and the great mistake is just to issue radios indiscriminately to people who have not been instructed in their use.

The people who obviously need to be on the net and will need to speak on it fairly frequently are:

> The announcer or chief commentator who will control it
> The trials director
> The technical delegate
> The president of the ground jury
> The chief steward
> The chief doctor
> The chief veterinary official
> The course builder (with one repair party for the marathon only)
> The second repair party (for the marathon only)
> The secretary (to communicate with the trials director when he is
>   not on the telephone)

The following could usefully 'listen out' on the net and be able to speak on it in an emergency:

> The ambulance crew (when the chief doctor is not with them)
> The second doctor
> The second (and other) veterinary officials
> The commentators who are out on the marathon course
> The stable manager (when away from his telephone)

The scorers
The person in charge of the public car parks (if not in contact by
    telephone)
Any steward who may be undertaking special duties

Communications throughout the marathon course will be well covered
by the administrative radio net and the wirelesses at the starts and
finishes of sections and at each obstacle, which can be used in
emergency.

Internal telephone lines should link the secretary's office with the
commentary box, the stable manager, the collecting ring, and possibly
the main gate and car park, the first aid tent, and the catering tent.

The final links in the communications system should be the main
score-board, and notice-boards at the secretary's office, the stable manager's office, the collecting ring and the finish of the marathon, on
which results as well as general notices may be posted.

These recommendations about communications amount to a counsel
of perfection which has hardly been achieved at any event in Britain or
abroad to date. Recent technical advances in the design of portable
radio transmitters, coupled with reductions in their cost and relaxa-
tions in British laws restricting their use, have made them entirely practical for instant accurate communication over a range of five miles.
However, this system will be workable only if used by people who can
understand the elementary principle that only one person can talk at a
time and are able to send their messages briefly and concisely.

One extra technical facility, 'bleepers' such as are used in big hospi-
tals to alert individuals when they are wanted on the radio and save
them having to listen to it all the time, will make the system completely
effective and virtually foolproof, and this is probably already available.

Timing Equipment

Timing equipment is essential for driving trials and up to a hundred
accurate, reliable clocks and stop-watches will be required for the
marathon day. In Britain these can be hired, together with all other
apparatus and paperwork needed, from the Driving Trials Group of the
British Horse Society, at an all-in cost which is lower than any which
could possibly be negotiated on the open market. The Group's clocks
are all electronic quartz digital ones which provide the best possible
guarantee of accuracy and the best possible assurance of their not being

misread by people who might easily mistake the position of the minute hand on a dial stop-watch. Three separate types are supplied to serve the different requirements of timekeepers, referees and obstacle judges respectively.

Electric-beam timing, as used for show jumping, is considered essential nowadays for the obstacle competition at national driving trials and its value is much reduced, and its cost largely wasted, if it does not incorporate a public display clock to keep spectators fully informed. The same system can be applied most effectively to individual marathon obstacles now that these have clearly defined entrances and exits. The timing is more precise when this system is used, and a display clock increases spectator interest, but cost and the difficulty of assembling enough sets seem likely to postpone indefinitely the time when it can be used for all obstacles. Meanwhile, the use of one or two sets for the more spectacular obstacles is a step in the right direction which has already been taken at several British events.

Flags, Markers and other Equipment

Apart from the dressage boards and markers and the cones, numbers, and other materials for the obstacle competition, a large number of red and white flags and direction arrows will be needed for the marathon course. This will vary considerably between courses but will never be less than fifty red and fifty white flags and fifty direction arrows, and may amount to two hundred of each. The red and white flags need to be stiff and with a surface on which numbers and letters can be written clearly but erased later. Clubs, groups and organisers generally will do well to assemble their own flags and arrows, and possibly their own dressage boards and markers.

White plastic guttering makes a good substitute for dressage boards. It is cheap, particularly if slightly damaged lengths, which are quite suitable for this purpose, can be bought, easier to lay out and stack for transport than boards, and does not blow over in a wind.

All the necessary equipment, together with an electronic weighbridge in sections, can be provided by the British Horse Society, who will send it in a large trailer which itself forms a superior score-board. All vehicles must be weighed at the end of a full five-section marathon under British national rules, but a weighing machine can be improvised from a large spring-dial suspended from scaffolding if distance or other factors preclude the cost of hiring the complete package.

John Richards, publisher of *Horse & Driving*, with his Hungarian cross Welsh Cob team in the unique setting of the Scottish event at Florrs Castle *(K. G. Ettridge, Horse & Driving)*

Official Cars

Although a welcome recent trend has been to reduce the number of motor vehicles, including official cars, driving over marathon courses and doing no good to their surfaces, some officials must have transport, particularly during the marathon, and will need four-wheel-drive vehicles to cope with the tracks.

These obviously include the trials director, the technical delegate, the course builder and any repair gangs working under him, the chief timekeeper, the chief steward and at least one doctor and one vet. The ground jury will need one, or possibly two cross-country vehicles to be under the control of their president for taking judges to and from their duties and for taking a quorum of them to marathon obstacles to hear objections *in situ*. There should be no need for organisers to provide

165

more official vehicles than these and timekeepers, obstacle judges, walk judges and other stewards or officials whose duties require them to be on the marathon course should generally be able to get to static positions in their own cars. Referees should be driven over the marathon course in official vehicles for a reconnaissance on the day before the marathon.

Provided that no damage to the track is envisaged, competitors cannot reasonably be forbidden to inspect the marathon course in their own vehicles at any time during the forty-eight hours before it is due to begin. It is difficult in practice to restrict the number of vehicles used by competitors for this purpose, and impossible to limit their trips round the course, but they can and should be banned from any parts of it which they are likely to damage, or from the whole of it if heavy rain makes most of it vulnerable. In this case competitors must approach the marathon obstacles to inspect them by the same routes as spectators.

Separate hard-surface routes must be planned to the compulsory halts and the areas of the obstacles for use by ambulances and veterinary vehicles as well as competitors' back-up teams. A trailer pulled by a good four-wheel-drive vehicle should be available as a horse ambulance with cross-country capability, and a low-loader with a similar towing vehicle may well be needed to recover wrecked carriages.

Catering

Catering is a major consideration which is invariably contracted to a professional firm. There are not very many of these in Britain with the capacity to operate independently under canvas for three or four days, and their popularity with competitors is a valid measure of their competence and should be studied in conjunction with their prices. A separate section reserved for competitors and officials should be provided if there is any possibility of their having to queue or wait for service.

At a well-established event a special refreshment tent for members can prove a popular facility and earn useful extra revenue; the more so in that 'subscriptions' will be paid in advance and not be affected by weather. It is a generous and inexpensive gesture to give free membership to competitors and officials.

Judges, stewards and officials and helpers who work throughout the trials understandably expect to be given free meals or refreshments. Most of these, however, have no time to sit down for leisurely luncheons and it is impractical and wasteful to give them vouchers which may only be exchanged for quick snacks worth a fraction of their value. At most continental horse shows such officials are happy to receive cash, but at driving trials in Britain it may be more appropriate to provide sandwiches and drinks for them in the director's, chief steward's and judges' tents on a self-help basis. The people concerned can be invited verbally to avail themselves of this privilege and will be unlikely to abuse it, and the drinks at least will be much cheaper than those bought from the caterer.

The Press

A press tent should be established at a big event. This should be permanently manned by a knowledgeable representative of the event and should contain tables and chairs, typewriters and two telephones, which can quite reasonably be coin-box operated. Coffee, sandwiches and drinks help to keep the press happy but can be sold, not given free.

A press handout should be available in this tent at the beginning of the trials and results should be posted promptly in it as soon as they are known. Photocopies of the actual score-sheets should be available at the end of each day, and copies of the final classification sheets should be provided without delay at the end of the event.

The Budget and Sponsorship

The financing of a driving event must always be a big headache for the organising committee. Its expenditure budget is subject to many variable factors but cannot really be less than £6,000 for a national three-day event in Britain, and may be as much as £30,000 for a big important trial run on largely commercial lines with little dependence on unpaid amateur workers or pure philanthropy from landowners and suppliers of material and equipment.

At least another £50,000 must be added to this to meet the costs of looking after foreign teams at World Championships, although most of this should be recovered through the gates from spectators. Sponsorship is the only realistic way of raising funds of this size and several firms, notably Famous Grouse Whisky and Norwich Union, have been very generous to British trials in this respect, while the British-based Wellcome Foundation was the prime sponsor of the 1984 World Championships in Hungary.

Commercial sponsorship is difficult enough to obtain, but when it is,

167

the conditions which it understandably seeks to impose to gain recognition and publicity for the sponsors must be carefully balanced against the interests of the competitors in their pursuit of a sport which is primarily and essentially an amateur one. With the exception of a few very good drivers in Eastern Europe who are employees of state studs, competitors cannot make their living by participating in driving trials and must indeed spend a great deal of their own money to do this. The prizes for which they drive seldom even cover their travel costs and, although they do not expect this and have never asked for prizes to be increased, their supreme contribution to the sport must never be underestimated. This, in the aggregate, would be beyond the resources of even the most generous sponsors, and the interests of drivers and their horses must never be put at risk by attempts, however well intended, to turn their competitive endeavours into public spectacles rather than tests of horsemanship.

10
Achievements and Prospects

'Don't worry, we can go faster than this!'

The International Scene

The international scope of driving trials, which was assured when the Duke of Edinburgh commissioned the international rules and established them under the authority of the International Equestrian Federation, gave them immediate status as a major equestrian sport and has added enormously to their interest, particularly in respect of the contacts which have been made through them with the countries of Eastern Europe. The horse truly knows no frontiers and the Iron Curtain has proved no barrier to the many drivers who have competed on each side of it every year and the several Englishmen who visit Hungary and Poland regularly on horse-buying expeditions. The United States of America have sent a good national team to each of the World Championships which have been held in years of even date since 1980, despite the enormous cost of flying their horses across the Atlantic.

The possibility of holding a true World Championship in America seems remote since few European nations could consider paying their own transatlantic travel costs. This has, however, been contemplated and may one day be achieved by flying the European teams from one or two airports in Europe at the expense of the host nation. Identical carriages could be built in America for the use of the European competitors and sold after the trials to cover their cost. The cost of such an enterprise would be enormous but might not be beyond the resources of American commercial sponsorship if interest in driving trials continues to grow there at its present rate.

Harness racing is very popular in Russia and competitions have been held there in the recent past which were not too dissimilar to our driving events. There are horses in Russia, notably the Orlov trotters, which would be ideal for competition driving, but to date the Russians have shown no interest in driving trials under the rules of the International Equestrian Federation.

Quarantine restrictions as well as travel costs prevent people bringing horses from Asia or Africa to compete in Europe, and driving trials enthusiasts in South Africa cannot really hope to compete outside their own country. The same situation affects the many keen competition drivers in Australia and New Zealand; these show great enterprise, however, in visiting Britain regularly without their horses, and inviting British drivers to visit them, so that their national trials conform closely to the pattern of the international ones. Several of these visits have been based on friendly events in which visitors have been lent horses with which to compete against their hosts.

It should be possible to duplicate the courses and conditions of a British event in a country in the southern hemisphere nearly enough to provide comparative results for at least a friendly international trial, provided that the same judges were to officiate at each of them. The marathon course and the sites for its obstacles would have to be uninterestingly flat so as to minimise the differences in gradients and going, but the marathon obstacles themselves and the obstacle driving course for Competition C could be of identical design in each country. Since an arrangement of this kind would limit the scope of the marathon

European and British National Champion Paul Gregory, a first class professional driver with an outstanding pair of Welsh Cobs *(Leslie Lane)*

course builder, the occasions on which it would be acceptable would be infrequent, but it might also serve to provide comparative results between single and tandem turnouts in different countries as well as the pony turnouts for which very few international events are available.

International Trials for Singles, Tandems and Ponies

There is a school of thought, particularly evident in Britain, which seeks the promotion of true international championships, including continental and world events, for all pony, tandem and single horse turnouts. Its adherents make the valid point that many such drivers

may be as skilful as those who drive teams and pairs of horses though they cannot afford to maintain a larger establishment. They urge that World Championships should be contested by national teams each consisting of a four-in-hand, a pair, a tandem, and a single turnout, and some of them suggest that a national team should consist of ponies as well as horses in each category.

This is an attractive idea which would provide admirable variety and enable more drivers to compete without increasing the number of horses involved. It would require the building of separate marathon obstacles, or even a separate marathon course, for the pairs and singles, which are so much shorter than the teams and tandems; but the greater number of entries would not necessarily need more days to be judged since two or three dressage arenas and dressage juries could be in operation concurrently. This idea is not likely to be favoured by the countries of Eastern Europe who have hardly any ponies and few tandem or single turnouts and, if such an event ever does take place, it will probably only be put on very occasionally as an addition to the normal international programme.

Revision of the Rules

The international rule book is to be revised and republished in 1986 with all the numerous amendments which have been made to it piecemeal since its last publication in 1982. The British national rule book will be revised and republished at the same time. These new rule books should go a long way towards clarifying the rules and making them more comprehensive and less liable to misinterpretation.

The standard of judging may be expected to improve accordingly and it must be said that there is room for this, particularly as regards decisions made about unusual occurrences during marathons. In their zeal to protect the reputation of the sport, some judges have displayed an understandable but undesirable tendency to exercise their authority more readily than their judgement and sought to award Draconian penalties for quite minor irregularities which the 1982 rule books do not take fully into account. They have sometimes created further confusion by attempting to misinterpret the intentions of rules to justify decisions they have made and, when this has failed, have fallen back on the pompous pronouncement that their decisions are final and irrevocable and they have a duty to impose discipline.

This concept is erroneous and may be offensive to competitors to

British National Champion David Brand with his Welsh Cob team. He has been National Champion since 1983, but such is the quality of our top drivers that he has not yet been claimed for a national team *(Findlay Davidson)*

whom it is applied. Although judicial opinions, as in the marks awarded for presentation and dressage, are not open to argument, decisions which a judge makes in interpreting and applying the rules must be upheld by a majority of his fellow jury members if they are to survive objections and even then may often be overruled by the appeal jury. Judges have no authority within their own rights to punish acts of misconduct or indiscipline which are not specifically covered by the rules, but must report these corporately as a jury to the national committee or the international federation.

Although the occasions on which the penalty of disqualification may be awarded are not fully covered by the international or British national rules, those which call for the penalty of elimination are, and they are precisely specified. Elimination is invariably mandatory and not left to the discretion of judges, so it should only be awarded under the direct authority of the rules and for an omission or infringement which may affect the outcome of the competition. Judges have been known to suggest on more than one occasion that a competitor who loses his hat or breaks his whip or uses foul language in an obstacle should be eliminated. This is absurd and can only bring the rules and thus the whole concept of driving trials into ridicule and disrepute.

Is the Marathon Hard on the Horses?

Some sensitive people who have watched the marathons of driving trials have criticised them for being hard on the horses, likely to cause injury to them and to their drivers and grooms, and generally indecorous or even unedifying. The intentions of these concerned spectators have nearly always been entirely kindly and their criticisms deserve consideration and reply.

Since the distances, speeds, and durations of marathons are precisely regulated by the rules, and the weights which the horses pull and the gradients and going which they encounter are planned and supervised and not just left to chance, they cannot vary widely and must all be either accepted or condemned. In a full marathon the horses are required to travel 27km in two and a quarter hours, equivalent to 17 miles at an average speed of 8mph. This, with no weight on their backs, is far less arduous than a good day's hunting and, because they are not required to gallop or jump, it is less strenuous than the second day of a ridden three-day event, or even than the cross-country phase of a one-day event. For these reasons, as well as the fact that the going is predetermined, they are far less liable to sprains and leg injuries than hunters or horses which jump fences in competitions.

Seventy years ago the Hungarian magnates regularly drove their favourite teams of four horses between Budapest and Vienna, a distance of 160 miles, in two days with one overnight stop, and paraded them in harness on the third day in sparkling show condition to the admiration of their friends. Driving trials simulate this practical demonstration of stamina, but to a far less demanding extent.

Since 1970, the records of driving trials reveal that two horses died of heatstroke after a marathon in very hot weather at a minor event in the South of France, and the four horses of a team were drowned in a river during a marathon in America. The latter incident led to an immediate international ruling that fencing must be erected to prevent horses straying into deep water at river crossings. No other fatalities or serious casualties are recorded anywhere in the world.

In British trials about three horses or ponies out of about one thousand which compete each year are retired by their owners because they become too tired to finish marathons. At the European Championships in France in 1979, the Dutch champion Tjerd Velstra, who won the World Championships three years later with a different team, retired his Friesian horses half a mile before the finish of the marathon, although they were leading in the event, because they all got tired and gave up in unison. High-couraged horses will work themselves to death given only moderate encouragement, but they cannot be coerced beyond their own willingness, and certainly not by a man armed with an implement no more punishing than a carriage whip.

Horses are certainly subject to mental stress during driving trials, as are their drivers, particularly when they are making frantic efforts to extricate themselves from marathon obstacles. However, the cynics who claim that driving trials are cruel because of the tedium and frustration which the dressage imposes on the horses and drivers as well as the spectators have a point which is about the only valid one in this context.

Human Injuries

No driver or groom has been injured at any British driving trial, up to 1985, to an extent which has kept him out of the game for longer than six weeks. The most serious casualty world wide to date has been the tragic injury, in the 1984 World Championships, to an Austrian groom, the owner of the team concerned, whose leg had to be amputated after it slipped between the spokes of a carriage wheel; there were no other casualties, human or equine, at those championships.

An estimate, which is really more a guess because no specific records have been kept of this, suggests that an average of one in twenty starters at any British driving trial is likely to turn over or fall out of the cart. This is lower than the average of falls in ridden horse trials but a carriage turning over is nearly always more dramatic than a horse and rider falling. The consequences are usually more serious and far reaching because the horses will often run away in panic dragging their upturned carriage and destroying it in the process, to the grave danger of bystanders who may be in the way.

Fortunately this has not happened very often and, in these circumstances, horses have usually been stopped before panic has set in. The more experienced and sophisticated horses have indeed often stopped of their own accord, apparently realising what has happened. At the British National Championships in 1984, Claudia Bunn's pony team actually finished the section and stopped in good order after doing so, although their driver and her two grooms and the referee were ejected from the carriage several hundred yards before this.

Horse psychologists who care to study driving trials will find ample evidence that horses have more sense than we usually credit them with and develop an awareness of the requirements of activities in which they are regularly involved to an extent which enables them to co-operate with their drivers through quite remote control, and sometimes with virtually none at all.

Driving Trials to the Rescue of Native Breeds

In the age of the motor vehicle the working horse is really redundant and his role is that of providing pleasure and recreation, mainly to people who want to ride. Most people like to ride a horse which is as nearly thoroughbred as may be consistent with their weight, or which has at least a preponderance of thoroughbred or Arab blood; and the growing number of people who ride competitively need in their horses the speed, or at least the scope in paces, which thoroughbred blood induces. The more stocky indigenous breeds of Europe and America, with more to offer by way of strength and substance than speed and elegance, were in decline, and even threatened with extinction in some cases, until their survival was secured by drivers who could make good use of characteristics in them which made little appeal to people who wanted only to ride.

Driving trials have confirmed the value of some of the qualities inherent in native breeds of horses and ponies other than those of high courage and absolute speed at which the thoroughbred, with its Arabian ancestry, excels. We need many, if not most, of these tough native breeds as foundation stock to breed back to when we want to infuse strength and substance into our more delicate modern riding horses. The Cleveland Bay, the Welsh cob, the Connemara and the Franches-Montagnes of Switzerland are typical examples of breeds which cross well with the thoroughbred to produce good riding horses but are more useful to drivers than riders in their pure states.

Since horses in harness must not jump fences and are not required to

Mick Flynn, driving Alan Bristow's Hungarian team in the World Championships, 1984. He was the highest placed non Hungarian competitor and as an expert professional coachman must have a brilliant future with these comparatively new horses *(Findlay Davidson)*

gallop fast for more than a few paces in driving trials, and since only relatively simple paces and movements are asked for in driven dressage, the physical abilities and experience of the horses which take part in them are relatively less significant than in any other competitive horse activities. A calm, bold temperament and a spirit of willing and intelligent co-operation are what a trials driver looks for more than anything else in his horses and if these qualities can be combined with good conformation and imposing or attractive 'presence', he can use his own skill and judgement to produce champions within two or three years. There are in fact very few driving trials competitors who can honestly feel that they have been denied top honours because their horses are not good enough.

A Sport for the Veterans

Driving trials make fewer physical demands on drivers than ridden trials do on riders. The increase in weight and the decrease in agility and physical fitness which most people suffer when they leave their youth behind them is far less significant for drivers than for riders. Very quick reactions are always important, but judgement and general horse sense born of experience more than compensate for any physical deterioration and even for some inevitable loss of nerve.

The late Mr Douglas Nicholson competed in a World Championship in his seventieth year and several successful national competitors have been over seventy-five years of age. Competition driving shares with ridden dressage the advantage of imposing virtually no upper age limit on its human participants, and only a very generous limit on its equine ones. By the same token people can start driving much later in life and still reach the top of the league, and a number of top-class drivers who have spent their earlier years in earning the money to be able to pay for their sport have done just this and brought great distinction to it.

Ride and Drive

It is a considerable help to a driver to be able to ride, if only for his own pleasure and not for competitive purposes, and parents will be well advised to insist on their children learning to ride before they learn to drive, or at least pursuing these two aims concurrently. However, some very good drivers cannot ride, notably Mr David Brand, the 1983 and 1984 British national champion, who has not yet had time to learn but is a great natural horseman and gained valuable experience for marathons in his earlier career as a motor-cycle trials rider, and Mr Alan Bristow who represented Britain several times in World and European driving championships, and also cannot ride, but has wonderfully quick reactions and excellent hand and eye co-ordination developed as an expert helicopter pilot.

Mr Alwyn Holder, one of our best international four-horse drivers, is a keen hunting man who learned to ride after taking up driving and he, like David Brand, discovered a flair for horsemanship through his children's ponies.

Driving provides an excellent means of keeping small ponies fit and in sensible work while children are at school and cannot ride them, and the same applies to hunters who benefit far more from working in harness with no weight on their backs from April until September than from being turned out in a field each summer. The driving trials season fits exactly into the one when there is no hunting, and the high proportion of driving trials competitors who hunt their horses during the winter find that the two activities complement each other wonderfully well. They get twice as much use and enjoyment from horses which are fitter, freer from lameness and illness, and generally more intelligently co-operative than those which are in work for only half of each year.

Of the five competitive horse sports which are controlled by the International Equestrian Federation and the national federations of each country, driving trials seem to be the fastest growing, at least in Great Britain. More than just performance trials for harness horses, although they have greatly enlarged the scope of carriage driving in this respect, they have added an extra dimension to horse sport and a new vista to the equestrian scene.

Appendix

The World Driving Championships

Münster (West Germany) 1972
Team medals: 1st Great Britain, 2nd Switzerland, 3rd Federal Republic of Germany
Individual medals: 1st Auguste Dubey (Switzerland), 2nd Sir John Miller (Great Britain), 3rd Douglas Nicholson (Great Britain)

Frauenfeld (Switzerland) 1974
Team medals: 1st Great Britain, 2nd Switzerland, 3rd Poland
Individual medals: 1st Sándor Fülöp (Hungary), 2nd Christian Iseli (Switzerland), 3rd George Bowman (Great Britain)

Apeldoorn (The Netherlands) 1976
Team medals: 1st Hungary, 2nd Federal Republic of Germany, 3rd Poland
Individual medals: 1st Imre Abonyi (Hungary), 2nd Emil Bernhard Jung (West Germany), 3rd Zygmunt Waliszewski (Poland)

Kecskemet (Hungary) 1978
Team medals: 1st Hungary, 2nd Federal Republic of Germany, 3rd Great Britain
Individual medals: 1st György Bárdos (Hungary), 2nd Sándor Fülöp (Hungary), 3rd Ferenc Muity (Hungary)

Windsor (Great Britain) 1980
Team medals: 1st Great Britain, 2nd Hungary, 3rd Poland
Individual medals: 1st György Bárdos (Hungary), 2nd George Bowman (Great Britain), 3rd Tjeerd Velstra (The Netherlands)

Apeldoorn (The Netherlands) 1982
Team medals: 1st The Netherlands, 2nd Hungary, 3rd Great Britain
Individual medals: 1st Tjeerd Velstra (The Netherlands), 2nd György Bárdos (Hungary), 3rd László Juhász (Hungary)

Szilvasvarad (Hungary) 1984
Team medals: 1st Hungary, 2nd Sweden, 3rd Great Britain
Individual medals: 1st László Juhász (Hungary), 2nd György Bárdos
(Hungary), 3rd Mihaly Balint (Hungary)

The European Driving Championships

Sopot (Poland) 1975
Team medals: 1st Hungary, 2nd Poland, 3rd West Germany
Individual medals: 1st Imre Abonyi (Hungary), 2nd György Bárdos
(Hungary), 3rd Ferenc Muity (Hungary)

Donaueschingen (West Germany) 1977
Team medals: 1st Hungary, 2nd Poland, 3rd West Germany
Individual medals: 1st György Bárdos (Hungary), 2nd Tjeerd
Velstra (The Netherlands), 3rd Emil Bernard Jung (West Germany)

Haras du Pin (France) 1979
Team medals: 1st Hungary, 2nd Great Britain, 3rd Poland
Individual medals: 1st György Bárdos (Hungary), 2nd Mihaly Balint
(Hungary), 3rd Zygmunt Waliszewski (Poland)

Zug (Switzerland) 1981
Team medals: 1st Hungary, 2nd Poland, 3rd Great Britain
Individual medals: 1st György Bárdos (Hungary), 2nd George
Bowman (Great Britain), 3rd Wladyslaw Adamczak (Poland)

The European Pairs Championships, Rome (Italy) 1983
Team medals: 1st Holland, 2nd Switzerland, 3rd France
Individual medals: 1st Paul Gregory (Great Britain), 2nd H. R. Pieper
(West Germany), 3rd Heine Merk (Switzerland)

The National Driving Championships

Year	Horse Teams	Pony Teams	Horse Pairs	Pony Pairs	Single Horse	Single Pony	Horse or Pony Tandems	Novice Horse	Novice Pony
1975	George Bowman	Joe Moore	Robert Blake	John Marson	Fred Harrison	Christine Dick			
1976	George Bowman	Vance Coulthard	Jim French	John Dick	Carol Dale	Claudia Bunn	David Morgan-Davies		
1977	Alwyn Holder	Ted Rowley	Richard Wilcox	Richard Wilcox	Tommy Fawcett	Mrs Blundell	A. Barnard		
1978	George Bowman	Albert Metcalfe	Christine Dick	Sydney Smith	Carol Dale	Deidre Colville	Robert Bowman		
1979	George Bowman	C. Barnard	Christine Dick	Claudia Bunn	B. Pattinson	Gay Russell	Robert Bowman		
1980	George Bowman	Karen Bassett	John Roger	David Hazeldine	Kate Maddocks	A. R. Brown	George Bowman Jnr		
1981	George Bowman	Karen Bassett	Paul Gregory	Mark Weston	Mrs J. Harrison	Amanda Waite	Les McRonald		
1982	George Bowman	Mark Broadbent	Paul Gregory	Gay Russell	Coupie Brown	Jill Neill	Timmy Robson	John Arden	Paul Boyle
1983	David Brand	Richard Margrave	Paul Gregory	Dick Beeby	Coupie Brown	Jill Neill	Timmy Robson	Ann Small	Mary Hamilton
1984	David Brand	Mark Broadbent	Mary Matthews	Diane Weston	Lyn Bourn*	Jill Neill	Tommy Fawcett	Helen Rogerson	Sue Noon

*Driving for John Ravenscroft

Overleaf HRH The Duke of Edinburgh and George Bowman in the closing ceremony of the 1984 World Championships *(Findlay Davidson)*

Bibliography and Further Reading

British Horse Society. *Horse Driving Trials National Rules* (1986)

Duke of Beaufort. *Driving* (Badminton Library, 1889)

Faudel-Phillips, H. *The Driving Book* (J. A. Allen, 1970)

Fédération Equestre Internationale. *General Regulations* (1986)

Gilbey, Sir Walter. *The Harness Horse* (Spur Publications, 1976)

HRH The Duke of Edinburgh. *Competition Carriage Driving* (Horse Drawn Carriages Limited, Macclesfield, 1982)

Howlett, Edwin. *Driving Lessons* (R. H. Russell & Son, New York, 1894)

Jung, Emil Bernard. *Combined Driving* (published in the USA, 1980)

Knight, C. Morley. *Hints on Driving* (J. A. Allen, 1970)

Norris, Anne and Pethick, Nancy. *Harnessing Up* (J. A. Allen, 1979)

Pape, Max. *The Art of Driving* (J. A. Allen, 1982)

Philipson, John. *Philipson on Harness and Nimshirich on Cape Cart* (Andrew Reid & Mawson, Swan & Morgan, Newcastle-upon-Tyne and Edward Stanford, London, 1882)

Rogers, Fairman. *Manual of Coaching* (J. B. Lippincott, Philadelphia, USA, 1900)

Ryder, Tom. *On the Box Seat* (Horse Drawn Carriages, 1969)

von Achenbach, Benno. *Anspannen und Fahren* (Germany)

von Felsödriethoma, Tibor Pettkó-Szandtner. *The Hungarian Driving Style* (ISKA Verlag AG, Zurich, Switzerland, 1984)

Walrond, Sallie. *Breaking a Horse to Harness* (Pelham, 1981)

——, (ed) *The Encyclopaedia of Driving* (Country Life, 1979)

——, *A Guide to Driving Horses* (Pelham, 1977)

——, *Your Problem Horse* (Pelham, 1982)

Ware, Francis *et al. Driving*

Watney, Mrs B. M. I. *The BDS Book of Driving* (British Driving Society, 1981)

Useful Addresses

British Horse Society
Horse Driving Trials Office
The British Equestrian Centre
Stoneleigh
Kenilworth
Warwickshire CV8 2LR
Tel: 0203–52441

The British Driving Society
27 Dugard Place
Barford
Nr Warwick CV35 8DX
Tel: 0926–624420

Hackney Horse Association
34 Stockton
Warminster
Wiltshire
Tel: 0985–50906

Horse & Driving
Gawsworth Court
Macclesfield
Cheshire
Tel: 02603–446/468

Horse and Hound
King's Reach Tower
Stamford Street
London SE1 9LS
Tel: 01–261 6315

Fédération Equestre Internationale
Schosshaldenstrasse 32
CH–3000 Berne 32
Switzerland

The Australian Driving Society
Karawera
Mansfield Road
Benalla
3673 Victoria

The Driving Digest Magazine of America
PO Box 467
Brooklyn
Connecticut 06234

Carriage Association of America
RD1
Box 115
Salem
New Jersey 08079

The American Driving Society
PO Box 1852
Lakerville
Connecticut 06039

The United States Equestrian Team Inc
Gladstone
New Jersey 07934

The New Zealand Driving Society
Alfriston Road
R. D. Manurewa
New Zealand

Index

'I repeat . . . you're off course!'

Numbers in *italics* refer to illustrations